The Star Road Map
Divination Beyond Time & Space

The Star Road Map

Divination Beyond Time & Space

4880 Lower Valley Road • Atglen, PA 19310

PATRICIA PADILLA &
MARLENA FREELOVE

Copyright © 2012 by Patricia Padilla and Marlena Freelove

Library of Congress Control Number: 2012945785

All rights reserved. No part of this work may be reproduced or used in any form or by any means—graphic, electronic, or mechanical, including photocopying or information storage and retrieval systems—without written permission from the publisher.

The scanning, uploading and distribution of this book or any part thereof via the Internet or via any other means without the permission of the publisher is illegal and punishable by law. Please purchase only authorized editions and do not participate in or encourage the electronic piracy of copyrighted materials.

"Schiffer," "Schiffer Publishing, Ltd. & Design," and the "Design of pen and inkwell" are registered trademarks of Schiffer Publishing, Ltd.

Designed by Danielle D. Farmer
Type set in Adresack™/EnviroD/ITC Kabel Std

ISBN: 978-0-7643-4222-6
Printed in China

Published by Schiffer Publishing, Ltd.
4880 Lower Valley Road
Atglen, PA 19310
Phone: (610) 593-1777; Fax: (610) 593-2002
E-mail: Info@schifferbooks.com

For the largest selection of fine reference books on this and related subjects, please visit our website at **www.schifferbooks.com**.
You may also write for a free catalog.

This book may be purchased from the publisher.
Please try your bookstore first.

We are always looking for people to write books on new and related subjects. If you have an idea for a book, please contact us at **proposals@schifferbooks.com**

Schiffer Books are available at special discounts for bulk purchases for sales promotions or premiums. Special editions, including personalized covers, corporate imprints, and excerpts can be created in large quantities for special needs. For more information contact the publisher.

In Europe, Schiffer books are distributed by
Bushwood Books
6 Marksbury Ave.
Kew Gardens
Surrey TW9 4JF England
Phone: 44 (0) 20 8392 8585; Fax: 44 (0) 20 8392 9876
E-mail: info@bushwoodbooks.co.uk
Website: www.bushwoodbooks.co.uk

Dedication

For our Ancestors with gratitude.
And for our daughters, Aponi & Marisol, our
greatest teachers in life and love.

Acknowledgements

Thank you, Melissa Weiner, for a home and encouragement. A big hug to Tracey Hagan, for schlepping our prototypes around; Carl Johan Calleman PhD, for his wonderful research; Lawrence E. Joseph and John Major Jenkins, who were great resources; and Madelena Morgan, who was a constant source of strength and encouragement.

Epigraph

We are born into community and exist in community.

We are part of the cosmos, surrounded by the Tree People, the Rock People, the Winged Ones, the Finned Ones, and the Creepy Crawly Ones.

We are affected by the stars and the planets, just as the oceans and winds are; and our Ancestors are always around us.

-Patricia A. Padilla

Contents

Chapter 1:
Unfolding *The Star Road Map* 10
   Description of *The Star Road Map* Cards ... 14
   World Tree 16
   The Fifth Element 18

Chapter 2:
Gods, Goddesses, and Glyphs 20
   00 Fool, Patecatl 23
   01 Magus, Quetzalpapalotl 25
   02 Priestess, Lady Xoc 27
   03 Empress, Chalchiuhtlicue 29
   04 Emperor, King Bird Jaguar 31
   05 Hierophant, Tezcatlipoca 33
   06 Lovers, Ometecuhtlis 35
   07 Chariot, Quetzalcoatl 37
   08 Adjustment, Law Giver 39
   09 Fortune, Maize God 41
   10 Lust, Tlazolteotl 43
   11 Hanged Man, Seven Macaw 45
   12 Death, Tzitzimitl 47
   13 Vision, Vision Serpent 49
   14 Devil, Earth Monster 51
   15 Tower, Fire/Water/Stream 53
   16 Star, Lamat 55
   17 Moon, Ix Chel 57
   18 Sun, Quetzalcoatl 59
   19 Stillness, Water Lily 61
   20 Universe, Teotihuacán Spider Woman ... 63
   21 Self Love, Xochiquetzal 65

Chapter 3:
First Father 68
   First Father, Emergence 71

Chapter 4:
The Cycle of Days 72
   Acceptance, 1 Day 76
   Expression, 2 Day 77
   Security, 3 Day 78
   Leadership, 4 Day 79
   Energetics, 5 Day 80
   Instinct, 6 Day 81
   Authenticity, 7 Day 82
   Moderation, 8 Day 83
   Persistence, 9 Day 84
   Authority, 10 Day 85
   Creativity, 11 Day 86
   Emotions, 12 Day 87
   Knowledgeable, 13 Day 88
   Wisdom, 14 Day 89
   Ambition, 15 Day 90
   Overcome, 16 Day 91
   Flexibility, 17 Day 92
   Share, 18 Day 93
   Curiosity, 19 Day 94
   Simplicity, 20 Day 95

Chapter 5:
Surfing the Overworlds 96
- Initiation, 1 Overworld 100
- Duality, 2 Overworld 102
- Action, 3 Overworld 104
- Stability, 4 Overworld 106
- Empowerment, 5 Overworld 108
- Flow, 6 Overworld 110
- Reflection, 7 Overworld 112
- Balance, 8 Overworld 114
- Patience, 9 Overworld 116
- Manifest, 10 Overworld 118
- Clarity, 11 Overworld 120
- Transformation, 12 Overworld 122
- Completion, 13 Overworld 124

Chapter 6:
Navigating the Underworlds 126
- Cellular, 1 Underworld 130
- Mammalian, 2 Underworld 131
- Familial, 3 Underworld 132
- Tribal, 4 Underworld 133
- Regional, 5 Underworld 134
- National, 6 Underworld 135
- Global, 7 Underworld 137
- Galactic, 8 Underworld 138
- Universal, 9 Underworld 140

Chapter 7:
The Four Directions 142
- North, MULUC 145
- South, CAUAC 146
- East, KAN 147
- West, IX 148

Chapter 8:
Divine Intercession 150
- Alchemy, Intercession 153
- Ancestors, Intercession 154
- Eclipse, Intercession 157
- Hand of God, Intercession 159
- La Reina, Intercession 161
- Nawal, Intercession 163
- Creation, Intercession 165
- White Flower, Intercession 167
- World Tree, Intercession 169

Chapter 9:
Hall of Mirrors 172

Chapter 10:
Reading the Map 176
- One-Card Reading 179
- Three-Card Reading 181
- Six-Card Reading 187
- Full Reading Using All 78 Cards 198

Conclusion 198

Endnotes 199

Bibliography 205

About the Authors Artists 207

Index 208

Chapter 1

Unfolding the Star Road Map

Description of *The Star Road Map Cards*

World Tree

The Fifth Element

According to the Maya, we are traveling along the Star Road, entering the belly of our universe. As we negotiate the cosmic winds and endure the thick cosmic dust on our way to the great cleft, or birthing place of the stars, we can thank the ancient stargazers for a road map.

Although we highlight and quote the Maya throughout this work, we are really incorporating many Mesoamerican tribes that used the 260-day sacred calendar with the 365-day solar calendar. The Mesoamerican era includes the Olmecs, Toltecs, Zapotecs, Maya, and Aztecs. One society has influenced the other, through a 22,000-year[1] time span. They had sacred calendars, ball games, architecture, gods, and blood sacrifice in common.

It is the Maya who speak the most eloquently and extensively about time, and are credited with the new math that produced such accuracy in calculating the movement of the planets. The Maya used the vestigial system, which was based on the number of fingers and toes or the number twenty.[2] With their system, they not only calculated the precise movement of the planets over trillions of years; but accurately predicted many singular events over the past millennia.

For those who have not been initiated into this world view, Star Road is the Milky Way, our own glorious and mysterious universe.

It is doubtful that there would be anyone academic or not, who would challenge the accurate observations and calculations made by the Maya about time and space. And how could anyone look at the Aztec calendar and not muse and get lost in the intricate and otherworldly symbology? As Lawrence E. Joseph notes in his book, *Apocalypse 2012*:

> ...It is a staggering intellectual achievement, equivalent in magnitude to ancient Egyptian geometry or to Greek philosophy. Without telescopes or any other apparatus, Mayan astronomers calculated the length of the lunar month to be 29.53020 days, within 34 seconds of what we now know to be its actual length of 29.53059 days. Overall, the 2,000-year-old Mayan calendar is believed by many to be more accurate than the 500-year-old Gregorian calendar we use today.

Who were these people and what more can we learn from them about our time and purpose on Earth? Why were the Maya so obsessed with time? Perhaps it is because they identified stable and predictable cyclical energies that emanated from the cosmos and affected Earth's physicality. Not only was their timekeeping impeccable, their prophecy of earthly events—wars, catastrophes, and agricultural concerns—were predicted accurately, generations ahead of the physical manifestation. The Maya, while charting time, were also glimpsing into future food supplies and world events that would affect their people. It is only through what remains of art and history that we get a clue as to how prophecy guided their lives.

At this time, through enhanced satellite imaging, archeologists and other scientists are re-exploring the site of El Mirador, Guatemala.[3] They have discovered the largest known pyramid on the planet. El Mirador was a cultural center as large as current-day downtown Los Angeles, California; and the sacred creation story of the Maya is carved into the walls of the pyramid. This is the first unedited version of the *Popol Vuh's* creation story of the Maya. It is hoped that a clearer picture of what they "saw" in the movement of the cosmos, so long ago, will shed light on the challenges we are facing today.

Even in the twenty-first century, researchers are still working feverishly to unwind the language of the Maya. Although we can decipher some of their history, carved into the glyphs that remain, we don't have the language to understand and appreciate the ideas they had about spiritual realities that pervade all matter here on Earth.

How can one not explore concepts like Quetzalcoatl or Nine Wind, the deity that pulls the sun's rays across heaven? And the pompousness of Lord 7 Macaw; and Huitzilopochtli, the left-handed hummingbird? One has to appreciate their lyricism and poetry about reality. While that may bring creatively minded people to the subject, the fact that through their calendar system, they could describe and predict World War I[4] is amazing.

If the Mayans had not been able to foretell the exact day for the arrival of the Spaniards, they would have lost their entire history. It was because they KNEW what energy that day was bringing forth, that they hid the surviving calendars and elders from destruction.[5]

We are only dealing with one of their many calendar systems in this deck. The Tzolkin (zol-KEEN) calendar is their sacred calendar which provides a unifying pattern of the Earth and cosmos. It continues to be the hub of their other calendars.

According to Carl Johan Calleman, PhD., the Tzolkin calendar is a pattern for an unfolding of creative energy. It is a tool for following the energies of the transformation of consciousness or the souls' evolution. Perhaps Calleman said it best in his book, *The Mayan Calendar and the Transformation of Consciousness:*

> Spirit is about to be recognized as primary to matter and yet inseparably connected with it.

In the Maya world view, the universe is seen as a web of creative interconnected energies of time and space on different hierarchical levels. This takes us right back to the Mayan elders who relate to Hunab K'u (WAN ab KWA), the "The One Giver of Movement and Measure, the Absolute Being, the Architect of the Universe." Mayan day keeper, Hunbatz Men, writes about, Hunab K'u, in his book, *Secrets of Mayan Science/Religion:*

> We believe, if we had access to the ancient day keepers, they would tell us that the planetary shift is a shift in consciousness; to a state of being that has no past or future. This consciousness reflects the presence and awareness of Hunab K'u, the One Giver of Movement and Measure, otherwise called the Great Spirit. In that concept, there is no separation; only unity with the infinite, creative mind we call, God.
> ~Hunbatz Men

Though the ice caps are melting and weather patterns are changing; though our economy is faltering and lifestyles are being altered; we are privileged to witness and experience what it means to be human and humble. More than that though, we are called to re-establish within ourselves, our connectedness to Hunab K'u or God.

The shifts we are experiencing can be a great and wonderful impetus to rediscover who we are individually, and collectively. It is with joy that we share with you, what we have been able to understand about the Mesoamerican world view. Each card has been hand drawn and interpreted as literally as possible, from the original art. For the reader, it is perhaps, a good way to begin an inward journey of awareness and gratitude as we face the many changes already in progress. We hope that your relationship to the cosmos develops through the use of these cards, and that it inspires you to love all of the transitions you are now experiencing.

Description of The Star Road Map Cards

The Star Road Map deck has been designed to reflect the mysterious and profound relationship the Mesoamericans have with the cosmos. Their concept of time, mathematics, and the calculations made in astronomy, have given us tools to use, to resonate more fully and consciously with the cosmos.

Since so much of Mayan history was destroyed during the Spanish conquest[6], we felt that the Aztec information would help us piece together a larger view of how the ancient Mesoamericans perceived reality. This, being reflected in the Aztec art and writings, is an added bonus for those who have been drawn into the mysterious web of information.

We have incorporated the generally accepted concept of the Major Arcana cards but adapted the meanings to include the Mesoamerican world view. There are no court cards or suites; instead, we have included the Days, Four Directions, Overworlds, Underworlds, and Intercession cards.

- The Day cards are energies to specific days.

- The Four Direction cards also carry a specific influence on the rest of the cards in the spread.

- The Overworld cards represent the cyclical cosmic or spiritual influences on physical reality and evolution.

- The Underworld cards are a depiction of what is known about our 16.4 billion year evolution.[7] It represents the maturation of the human brain from amoeba to co-creators with Hunab K'u.

- The Intercession cards represent intervention by Creator.

It is the interaction of all of these energies that begins to create a multidimensional picture of the energies affecting ourselves and Mother Earth in the past, present, or future.

However, if you consider that they were describing current events thousands of years ago, we begin to understand the concept of the eternal present moment. It is through the prophetic writings of many ancient cultures that we can begin to grasp the meaning of "no time." It is not a new concept, nor should it be a scary one.

The mathematical precision used by the Maya to describe the movements of the observable planets, was matched only by their ability to describe a concept called "precession of the equinoxes."[8]

Precession is the way in which the Earth wobbles on its axis as it orbits our sun. It is in their description of this movement, where the Maya are astoundingly precise in their description of the energies encountered in the universal movement of our planet. Every degree of tilt or forward movement through our solar system moves us through different energies in the cosmos. Like modern-day astrologers, the Maya used their own symbols to describe what energies would be encountered at very specific times.

It is the prophetic and accurate description of these energies encountered throughout our history that has captivated the imagination of modern day scientists and scholars.

Comparative studies done on the Mayan calendars and the historical events of our planet have been wildly accurate, though predicted thousands of years in advance. The same symbols used then, are incorporated into *The Star Road Map* deck, to encourage you to dance with the mystery of our collective journey through the universe.

Carl Johan Calleman's book, *The Purposeful Universe*, is perhaps the best reference to identify historical events of the past several thousand years that were predicted and described by the Maya stargazers long before the events occurred.

Many of Maya/Aztec deities have a dual function in describing physical and spiritual reality, so do not be confused when you come across the same names in different segments of the deck. The differing ideas will be elucidated in the text, which you will come to know as you explore these ancient ideas and concepts.

Our humble effort to emulate their art is our desire to keep their vision of essence and beauty alive. We do not claim to understand or have a handle on the knowledge of the early Mesoamericans, but rather celebrate what little has been preserved and is still being discovered.

World Tree

The World Tree symbol is highlighted here because it represents the energetic "glue" or thread that defines our universe and gives us our concepts of time and space. The World Tree connects us to other universes that we haven't yet discovered.

This energetic configuration, identified by the ancients in many cultures thousands of years ago, is the generator of the concept of time and space. Astrophysics is now attempting to give a new language and description to the World Tree of the ancients. Through studies of cosmic dust, the numerical analysis of temperature variations has shown cohesive patterns emanating from the cosmic "Big Bang" of 15 billion years ago.[9]

As Carl Johan Calleman argues, this creates a dilemma for those who believe our universe is a random happening. It suggests, rather, that there is a grand design that is beginning to emerge with more complexity than previously thought. These numerical models are showing a vortex of energy that spans a distance a million times larger than our own Milky Way. These satellite measurements taken in 2003 suggest a "central axis" or a World Tree idea that is the energetic "glue" that holds our universe in sync with other universes yet to be discovered.[10]

Present day astronomers are validating what the Maya knew thousands of years ago. We are "holographic resonances"[11] of the energetic activity that created our universe.

Time is the movement of the identifiable planets and the movement of our own planet, measured against the stationary position of the Milky Way. Although everything is in perpetual motion, this is our contrast and form of measurement.

Where astrologers use the movement of our planet in and out of constellations to gauge different energetic patterns, the Mesoamericans used our movement gauged by universal proportions to define and describe the spiritual energies encountered on our journey through the stars.

We can look at the concept of time in many ways. There is secular time, which is a schedule for the mechanistic movements that define our existence, or sacred time which is about the movement and evolution of our consciousness.

We used to be farmers and shepherds. Time had a different meaning when we considered the most opportune moment to plant seeds or arrange our flocks for optimal reproduction.

Today is different, we are separate from the rhythms of the cosmos with electric lights, artificial schedules, and lives that are too busy to even notice the beauty of a sunset or sunrise.

It is only during times of chaos and crisis that we stop the grind and machinations of this precarious and false construct. While most people operate on a secular schedule, the ancient Mesoamericans lived by a spiritual time frame.

While in the Western world, we follow the 365-day Gregorian calendar, we design holidays and time schedules that serve commerce. The Maya designed their 260-day Tzolkin calendar to observe the spiritual influences we encounter as we travel the Star Road.

We mark our calendars, set our watches, and focus everything around making money. That is secular time. When one witnesses the birth of their child, the world is forever changed. Time stands still, as an old spirit enters a new body and, in an instant, transforms your identity and purpose. This is an example of sacred time. As we get ever closer to the dark rift or birthing place of the stars and our galaxy, we will be more intimate with sacred time. As we "shift" with our Mother Earth, the sacred will be all that matters.

Consider this time as a return to source. Geographically, we are approaching the birthing place of our own sun and planetary system. It is a time when we are reuniting with Creator, Hunab K'u. This is where contrast will not serve us anymore, up and down; right and wrong, black or white, or smart and stupid. We are one.

Let us move through these ethers with clarity, that what is good for one is good for all. We can no longer justify division or conflict.

The Maya, and indeed most of Mesoamerica, resonated with sacred time which was characterized by their pantheon of deities.

The Fifth Element

According to Carlos Barrios, Mayan elder from the Mam tribe of Huehuetenango Guatemala, we are encountering a new element: ether. This unseen force is a powerful medium that pervades the cosmos and the earth and can accommodate a wide range of frequencies.[12]

As Barrios suggests in his writing and lectures, the "new" fifth element is yet to be discovered. Perhaps it is like everything else, the element, called "ether" by the ancient Maya, is not new; but rather, we are just now developing a capacity to recognize its import in the realm of physical experience. It would make sense as we think about how the Maya described and charted the evolution of human consciousness over the past 16.4 billion years.

Interestingly enough, researchers from Stanford and Purdue Universities are suggesting the sun might be emitting a previously unknown particle that is meddling with the decay rates of matter. Or, at the very least, we are seeing some new physics yet to be defined and described by our observation and experience.[13]

In the scientific realm, radioactive decay rates have always been a predictable and constant value. However, scientists are discovering that the methodology of dating ancient artifacts by the use of carbon 14 dating is no longer accurate. The decay rate is becoming variable instead of constant. Oncologists are also facing a dilemma as they find that radiation treatments and some forms of chemotherapy are not as reliable as they once were.

Peter Sturrock, professor emeritus of applied physics at Stanford University, believes that there is a possibility that this unexpected shift could be related to activity at the core of our sun, 93 million miles away. When we can recognize what is causing the variation in decay rates, it will necessitate rewriting and reformulating how we look at physical reality.[14]

And at the same time, astrophysicists are identifying a new substance being emitted from the sun called "plasma." Could either of these be the new element? And as the new energetic is effecting the heavy metals on earth, can it be that it is also affecting our DNA? Perhaps this is part of a final step in the evolution of human consciousness where we realize that the respiration of the sun affects our own; perhaps we can no longer convince ourselves that the solar winds don't affect us and that the suffering on the other side of the planet doesn't either.

HEBIX U TOP'OL NEKE, HEBIX U HOK'OL YALCHE Y TIP'IL LOL
As the seed buds, as the flower emerges and blossoms

BEYO HEBIX U ZIHIL LE WUINICE.
In this way is born the human being.

BEL U YUCHUL TU LACAL TU K'AB HUNAB K'U
In this way, everything occurs in God's hands.

CALANTEN IN HUNAB K'U, CALANTEN!
Take care of me, Giver of Movement and Measure
Take care of me!

~Hunbatz Men
from *Secrets of Mayan Science/Religion*
Artwork by Patricia A. Padilla

Chapter 2

Gods, Goddesses, and Glyphs

0 Fool, Patecatl
1 Magus, Quetzalpapalotl
2 Priestess, Lady Xoc
3 Empress, Chalchiuhtlicue
4 Emperor, King Bird Jaguar
5 Hierophant, Tezcatlipoca
6 Lovers, Ometecuhtli
7 Chariot, Quetzalcoatl

8 Adjustment, Law Giver
9 Fortune, Maize God
10 Lust, Tlazolteotl
11 Hanged Man, Seven Macaw
12 Death, Tzitzimitl
13 Vision, Vision Serpent
14 Devil, Earth Monster
15 Tower, Fire/Water/Stream

16 Star, Lamat
17 Moon, Ix Chel
18 Sun, Quetzalcoatl
19 Stillness, Water Lily
20 Universe, Teotihuacán Spider Woman
21 Self Love, Xochiquetzal

We have used twenty-two (22) of the Mesoamerican deities as the archetypical images. They represent the Mesoamerican world view and are used to describe the energetic influences of a reading.

For the Maya, science and religion were inseparable. Through the practice of ritual, bloodletting, divination, and celebration, the ancients kept their world in harmony.

Deities represented spiritual energies that influenced the daily lives of the people. It was the duty of the ruling class to be intermediaries between the gods and the people. They would routinely make blood offerings and seek visions to commune with the gods.

Although there are many gods within the pantheon of Mesoamerican deities, there is only one supreme entity with many faces. Ometeotl, the "Dual Divinity," is the embodiment of opposites within one godhead. Ometeotl was a bisexual god with a female counterpart ruling the nine Underworlds. That face of the supreme deity was known as "Lord and Lady of the Land of the Dead." All else was but illusion.[1]

Ometeotl presided over a multi-layered universe, dwelling in the thirteenth heaven, far above other celestial activity such as the wind and moon and stars. Beneath the heavens, there existed a layered underworld through which the souls of the dead had to pass. Mictlan Opochalocan, or the "Land of the Dead, Where the Streets Are on the Left," was a perilous journey for the souls of the dead.[2]

Many of the deities are representational of the elements: earth, air, fire, water, and wind. Other gods have to do with agricultural powers or challenges. Some deities are representational of the Nawal spirit that accompanies every individual soul. In the final analysis, each god is a face of the "One Giver of Movement and Measure," or Hunab K'u.

Each card that we have created for the Major Arcana is a different face of Divine Intelligence.

0 Fool
PATECATL

Key: Creativity.

Inspiration: Deconstructing the false boundaries that allow us to think we are separate from creation.

Energetic: Exhibits the true strength and courage of a seeker who longs for union and wholeness with Creator. This card can indicate the desire to expand consciousness to accommodate greater understanding of what it is to be alive spiritually and physically. For those in the healing or teaching profession, it can be a grave error to think that you alone have an answer to any of the questions that life can present. It is a wise practitioner that will be open to guidance from the sacred in finding answers.

Goal: Work and play with an intention of achieving an open channel to the Sacred. Be curious and open to learning new things about what you think is real.

Light: This card can indicate an openness to change that would only be expansive and beneficial. It carries a joyful sense of adventure.

Shadow: When one moves through the world without consciousness, there can be a great deal of wreckage and destruction. It is wise to revise travel plans and figure out where you want to go and why.

History: Patecatl (Pah-te-CAH-tl) is the Aztec god of medicine.[3] He is known as the god of pulque, an alcoholic beverage made from the maguey plant and honey. Patecatl was also the discoverer of peyote, and with his wife, Mayahuel, he was the father of Centzon Totochtin (Four Hundred Rabbits), the divine rabbits and god of drunkenness.[4]

Patecatl symbolizes for our purposes, a being that is able to suspend his earthly ideas and visit another perspective by changing dimensions through the use of pulque or peyote. In this sense, drunkenness, achieved in the medicinal/spiritual sense, can help us suspend our prejudices and see a person or situation from a wider perspective.

It is through these circumstances of letting go of our limited understanding, which we can often grow to accommodate a larger, more sacred perspective. There are many ways of letting go. One can change professions because Spirit bids it; one can change residences and dare to create new community when their living situation grows stale; or we can choose another way of perceiving what we think robs us of our joy. It is in identifying and taking responsibility for our discomfort that can be the impetus for our greatest growth and adventure.

In indigenous societies, peyote and other hallucinogens are used to cure mental, spiritual, and physical illness. The substances are usually introduced through a sacred ceremony by a medicine person who has a profound relationship and understanding of the substance used. In contemporary times, it is a fool who engages these allies without understanding the nature and spirit of the substance.

As we move our consciousness from the realm of physicality to spiritual awareness, we no longer have need for substances. This is a good time to connect with the indelible Spirit thread that connects us to Creator.

0 Fool
PATECATL

I Magus
QUETZALPAPALOTL

Key: Transformation.

Inspiration: It is time to recognize that you too are a magician and can mold and transform any reality at hand by changing your perception of it. Do not rely on someone else to identify who and what you are. You have the power to manifest what you desire.

Energetic: The use of will to progress the souls' evolution according to divine plan. This card indicates the vital energy for transformation and suggests that we, like the butterfly, are at times in a larvae state deciding whether or not to let our wings unfold. The information and ability for flight is there, it is our will that determines whether we will fly or not. All that you need is available. Where is your will and what would you choose and why?

Goal: Your intention is to dance with the physical world as though you realize that you have the power to transcend any obstacle. Use your power for evolution and enlightenment. As you allow your wings to unfold, be conscious of where the newfound mobility can take you. If you feel stuck, change your perception of the situation, and how you relate to it.

Light: The evolution of the soul is an act of indescribable beauty and strength that serves the cosmos.

Shadow: You may be stuck in an unsightly cocoon, longing for fresh air and mobility. If this is causing you grief and frustration, remember that you have everything you need for transformation. Even in a jail cell, imagination cannot be contained.

History: Quetzalpapalotl (ket ahl PAH pah low tl) is the "Butterfly god."[5] Although little information remains about this god of transformation, there is a palace built in his honor in Teotihuacán.[6] The image speaks to us of change and transformation on the deepest levels of physical and spiritual existence.

This image suggests the energy of a magician, one who serves by showing us many forms and manifestations of the same reality.

Isn't it magic that we can evolve from sperm and egg into fully grown adults and then transform again into the "no-thing state" of etheric existence. It is as if the magician can play in both the Underworld and Overworld and present a face for eternity in the Middleworld (Earth). We are always on the precipice of evolving into yet another divine expression of Creator. There is nothing that can interfere with this potential, except our own will.

I Magus
QUETZALPAPALOTL

2 Priestess
LADY XOC

Key: Guidance.

Inspiration: The idea informing and designing matter is unlimited. As Spirit informs matter, it strives to inform our consciousness. If we are truly "conscious," then it is because we allow the Infinite to guide, with every breath, every thought and every action.

Energetic: The Priestess is able to traverse universes by stepping outside of the conscious mind and the shackles of the five senses. She avails herself to Creator by stopping her thought process and becoming an open channel for cosmic/divine energy. In doing this practice (prayer, ritual, bloodletting, etc.), she becomes a conduit for transformative guidance and understanding. If this card appears in your spread, it could be a suggestion to stop trying to think or rationalize your way through the issue and rely on the Infinite for direction. Perhaps the circumstance is larger than your understanding and the answer needs to be larger than the circumstance.

Goal: Clarity is always the best answer to any problem or concern. Beneath what appears as chaos and confusion, is often a brilliant truth that can further the souls understanding of all things. This card would indicate that one needs to step aside and humbly ask for guidance from Creator for right action, clearer vision, and understanding.

Light: It is a wise person who knows when it is time to stop talking and thinking. Often, it is most beneficial to still ourselves, call on a higher power, and be alert to the many forms of information and guidance that permeate the Middleworld. When we can learn to access this information, we become true alchemists.

Shadow: It is time to let go of the physical realm. Stop pretending as though you have all the answers. Initiate quietude; listen to the breath of the Divine.

History: Lady Xoc (Shoke) was a Mayan Queen Consort in Yaxchilan and is considered to have been one of the most powerful and prominent women in Mayan civilization. She was the principal wife of King Itzamna Balham III, "Shield Jaguar the Great," who ruled Yaxchilan from A.D. 681 to 742.[7]

In the depiction of Lady Xoc on our card, we see the pinnacle of the blood sacrifice with the Vision

Serpent rising above her. She is perhaps seeking help from the gods as her husband prepares for battle; or perhaps asking the ancestors for help in ministering to her people. We use her as the Priestess because she is traversing the worlds to receive guidance from beyond the "veil" to address earthly matters.

> As a result of Lady Xoc's blood sacrifice, a vision serpent rises from a bowl that rests on the ground. Vision serpents were apparitions of great rearing snakes that became manifested through bloodletting rituals. Ancestors, deities, and nobles were materialized from the mouths of such ethereal serpents. In the scene in Lintel 25, the bloodletting ritual has opened communication with the other worlds, and the bloodletting bowls function as an ol, or portal, through which the vision serpent passes into the Middleworld.[8]

The evolutionary process, that we are all subject to, has changed the way in which we access "otherworldly" information. We can now offer a prayer, focus our intent, and meditate to access the same information. Gone are the days, when we had to traumatize ourselves to "travel across the veil" or to access the subconscious mind. If you have drawn this card, it is a suggestion to look beyond the illusion for additional information.

2 Priestess
LADY XOC

3 Empress
CHALCHIUHTLICUE

Key: Compassion.

Inspiration: The Empress card, depicting the earthly mother, is a reminder that a woman can birth, nurture, and sustain any manner of humanity. It is through the love and nurturing of a mother, within the womb and after, that we are afforded the opportunity for evolution on the physical plane.

Energetic: The Empress card represents the earthly mother as a replica of the Great Goddess. To birth a child is to take the unseen energies of the universe and recreate a Divine idea in the physical form of a child. The Empress is a conduit through which selfless love manifests in the form of substance (mothers' milk), compassion, and understanding. Sheisstrong, durable, and a conduit for the infinite.

Goal: If this card appears in your reading, it is a signal to look at the issue or situation with the wisdom and compassion of the Empress. Serving as a conduit for compassion and selfless love, can and will, advance your efforts in any situation. When we love in this manner, we remove ourselves as targets of misunderstanding.

Light: There is no higher calling on the planet than that of a mother. She births us, nourishes us, and gives of her substance to insure our survival. Mother Nature is the prime example of this. If this card falls in a beneficial place in your reading, you are contributing to the balance and beauty of the planet.

Shadow: Think of the failed opportunities to love and understand, and you may have a good idea of how a situation can go wrong. If this appears in a poorly dignified position, you may be stuck in judgement and ridicule.

History: Chalchiuhtlicue (chahl chee oo TLEE kway) is the Aztec water goddess, the patron of newly born children[9], deity of the oceans, lakes, rivers and streams, and consort of the rain god, Tlaloc.[10] She was also referred to as "She of the Jade Skirt" or "She Whose Night-Robe of Jewel-Stars Whirls Above."[11] Chalchiuhtlicue was the ruler over the previous Fourth Sun which was destroyed by floods.[12]

3 Empress
CHALCHIUHTLICUE

4 Emperor
KING BIRD JAGUAR

Key: Fairness.

Inspiration: No matter where this card appears in your reading, it will always be about justice, balance, and wisdom. No matter who it may pertain to in your reading, it ultimately pertains to the internal "father" energy you carry within your own consciousness. How many times have you seen women marry the controlling, critical "father," repeatedly; or men who keep finding tyrannical bosses? If this is your experience of authority, it is time to renegotiate your understanding of the internal father.

Energetic: Levity, kind governance, balance around physical order, and protection of the real would be a few words to describe the idea of an Emperor.

Goal: In order to deal with the uncertainty and chaos of physical existence, we look for a stabilizing force in our daily challenge of facing the unknown. We honor justice and balance and strive for an orderliness that can be the foundation of all else.

Light: If this card appears in your reading, it could certainly indicate that there are father issues to be conscious of. In a good position, it could speak of a job well done, for you or by you. It could be indicating that the job you are doing in your home or workspace is in balance.

Shadow: The Emperor in a poorly placed position in a reading could indicate someone who is critical, controlling, and full of judgment. This could indicate someone who is dealing strictly from the head with no connection to the heart.

History: Palenque appears to have risen to its zenith under King Pacal (AD 615-83).[13] Although he inherited the throne from his mother's lineage at the age of twelve[14], it was during King Pacal's rule, that Palenque attained greatness in the region and thrived. His mother, Lady Zac-Kuk, lived another twenty-five years after his ordination.[15] King Pacal left many inscriptions and landmarks during his reign.

When we think of the Emperor, we think of the wise man who rules with wisdom and equanimity. We see in our mind's eye, the archetypal image of a good father, capable of unconditional love and kindness, one who could rule a kingdom in a way that benefits the entire kingdom.

The Emperor or "good father" figure is what all of us long for throughout our lives: someone wise, strong, and good who can give us protection and good council. It is possible, but it first has to begin with us. What is our identification of good, kind, and wise? How does that look in our reality? These are the answers within that will lead us to this energy.

4 Emperor
KING BIRD JAGUAR

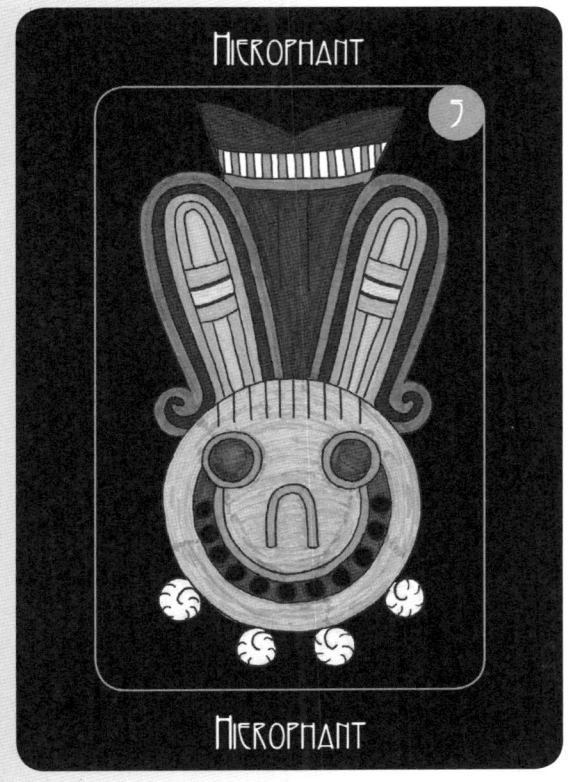

5 Hierophant
TEZCATLIPOCA

Key: Hidden Truth.

Inspiration: In any position, the Smoking Mirror is a reflection to us that we would benefit from discerning truth from fiction. It is hard work to let go of false ideas that cloud our thinking. We often persist with false ideas because it often justifies behavior that is habitual, or requires less of us. When we dare to look inside and find our truth, we become authentic and powerful. Dare to discover who you really are, the world will respond. Truth is the hallmark of personal power.

Energetic: The image of Smoking Mirror suggests a search for hidden truth, the quest for reconnection with Creator, through truth. If this card appears in a reading, look for the deeper meaning of your experience. Question and be prepared to surrender opinions for a greater understanding of the issue.

Goal: When this card appears, it beckons us to dig beneath the surface of the issue and find the truth about who we are in this circumstance. Are we acting out of integrity or just acting?

Light: The well-placed version of this card is that we are connected to the truth of the matter and can act from our highest good to transform any situation. It suggests that we may be able to shed the light of truth on the situation with beneficial results.

Shadow: If Smoking Mirror shows in a poorly dignified position, it would be a warning to bring the issue into full sunlight to correct misunderstanding. If it comes up in a negative way, it indicates that there is arrogance and falseness surrounding the issue.

History: Tezcatlipoca (tes kah tlee POH kah), was a principal god of rulers, sorcerers, and warriors.[16] The "Lord of the Smoking Mirror" wore a volcanic glass obsidian mirror in the back of his head or in place on one foot. Used for its reflective properties, he could "see the patterns of the future and the private imaginings of people's hearts."[17] It was thought that the emblems of Tezcatlipoca would enable priests and kings to peer into the souls of the people they served or encountered. Tezcatlipoca was a deity of war and signaled a "cycle of destruction and new creation."[18] For our purposes, we have chosen Smoking Mirror to represent the traditional Hierophant idea because of the deity's ability to see beyond the physical into the souls of men. Smoking Mirror is about hidden truths. This energy is about a known, but unproven higher order, which we are all a part of. According to scholars Karl Taube and Mary Miller, *The Gods and Symbols of Ancient Mexico and the Maya*, Tezcatlipoca or Smoking Mirror" appears to be the embodiment of change through conflict."

5 Hierophant
TEZCATLIPOCA

6 Lovers
OMETECUHTLIS

Key: Love.

Inspiration: The truest inspiration one can bring to a relationship of any kind is to have cultivated an appreciation of life that is joyful and infectious. When you love yourself and the life you have created, it is much easier to love another.

Energetic: This card presents the idea that the energy for love is present and challenges us to move beyond the illusion that another can grant us union with the infinite. If this card shows up in a reading, you may be longing for another to appear. If you are in a relationship, you may be waiting for your beloved to become more intimate. Until you can become more intimate with yourself, without desiring more, you cannot establish that with another.

Goal: The idea is to become whole within ourselves. Then and only then is it possible to have success as a lover.

Light: When this card appears in your reading, it could indicate that there is an interaction with another who has taken place or is about to take place. Strive to act from your strength and deep understanding. You are lovable and complete within yourself.

Shadow: In a challenged position, this card would indicate that you are unsure of yourself. You are too afraid of rejection to act in an authentic manner. Seeking re-assurance from another can cause the relationship to falter. Self acceptance and love can only come from within you. Back up and regroup.

History: In the Nahuatl/Aztec tradition, Ometecuhtli (oh may tay COO tlee) /Omecihuatl (oh may SEE wahtl) is a dual god, male and female.[19] In *Aztec Thought and Culture*, Miguel Leon-Portilla interprets this as "Lord of Duality."

When we think of the Lovers card, it usually inspires a deep hope and longing within us that it will herald a strong, enduring connection. We hope for a partner whose energy can flow with ours and act as the ultimate compliment to our existence. We have an innate longing to "become one," with another.

Here we put a new nuance on the Lovers card. In the depiction of Ometecuhtli, the god of duality, we suggest that our idea of a lover, too often, is about what they can bring to us or vice versa. The idea is a good one, in the world of separation and duality.

For the purposes of the "paradigm shift" that we are experiencing, it would better serve us to realize that our "lover" is within each of us. Ultimately, it doesn't matter who the beloved is, if we do not carry that completion within ourselves.

This card, in a reading, can indicate that another is either present in your life as a lover, or about to arrive in your universe. Let this card remind you, that love is bigger than any differences or separation. Let it be a reminder for you, of union rather than separation. Love is a gift, a grace. One cannot conjure nor create it like a meal or a piece of clothing. It is rather, a frequency, that we resonate to; or not. Choose to let go of self scrutiny and insecurity and bask in the expansive opportunity for extending your community and family.

6 *Lovers*
OMETECUHTLIS

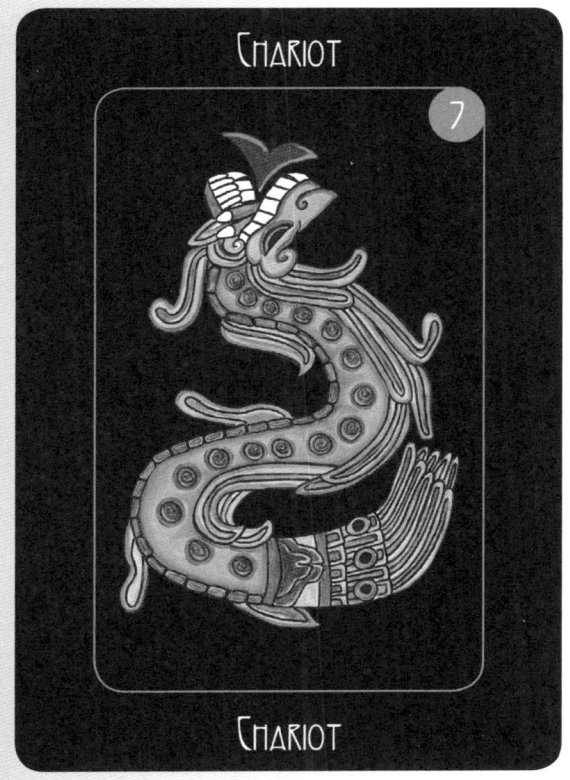

7 Chariot
QUETZALCOATL

Key: Movement.

Inspiration: Throughout every culture and its history, we learn of the cyclical death and rebirth of all things. We are no different. What challenges us one day, serves to strengthen and clarify our brilliance the next. Dare to move; you are that phoenix rising and Quetzalcoatl is with you.

Energetic: This card in a reading would indicate you are indeed in a transition that could indicate greater freedom, mobility, and awareness. It is as if you are recognizing that you may have been incarcerated behind a fence, but there are no locks on the gate. You have an opportunity at this time, to free yourself from concepts, people, and things that have diminished your growth and creativity.

Goal: Standing at the edge of the precipice, we shudder in fear that we cannot fly. It is our fear that incarcerates us. Extend your arms, marvel at your own gossamer wings and let the breath of Creator carry you to your destiny. Trust yourself and be grateful.

Light: This card indicates that you have laid the foundation for your own growth and expansion. Continue in your forward movement and do not look back at what might have been. It is your own innate wisdom that brought you to this precipice of change.

Shadow: If this card falls in a challenging position, you are choosing to view the reflection rather than the source of light. Take a deep breath and stop avoiding your potential.

History: Kukulcan (Koo KOOL kahn) is the Yucatec term for the Aztec god Quetzalcoatl (ket sahl KO ahtl). We have chosen Quetzalcoatl, the Feathered Serpent (from Nahuatl *quetzalli*, "tail feather of the quetzal bird [*Pharomachrus mocinno*]," and *coatl*, "snake")[20] to represent the idea of the chariot, because of his role in Mesoamerican mythology. Kukulcan or Quetzalcoatl is the patron god of the priesthood of learning and knowledge.[21] This card represents higher level movement. It suggests grace and elegance.

Quetzalcoatl weaves in and out of Mesoamerican history as the god that drags the sun's rays across the darkened sky, chasing night to the Underworld and illuminating the heavens at night, as the morning star. Like the phoenix rising, he suffers humiliation and destruction, only to resurrect and journey to the Underworlds to retrieve the broken bones of the ancestors. With the help of the Cihuacoatl, the broken bones are ground into flour, moistened with Quetzalcoatl's blood, and shaped into human form.[22]

It is said that Quetzalcoatl, as the planet Venus, can exhibit maligning influences, lending energy to poor weather and an influence for war.[23] As the Tolpiltzin Quetzalcoatl of Tollan, he was known for refusing to sacrifice human beings, and instead, his offerings were always snakes, birds, and butterflies.[24]

In our own earthly experience, we move from our own heaven and hell like the deities in Mesoamerica. Each time we traverse these realms, we learn more about our attitudes and the decisions we make. We learn that no action is a decided action; and renew with each challenge the spark of evolution. We are no different from the stars and the planets. We are held in our orbits by a Divine Architect, who oversees our journey to completion and perfection.

7 Chariot
QUETZALCOATL

8 Adjustment
LAW GIVER

Key: Honor.

Inspiration: Even contemporary lawmakers and givers will admit that man-made law has little to do with justice. The only hand in the universe with levity is that of Hunab K'u, or Creator. Right action and thinking is the foundation for balance. Truth is power.

Energetic: There are issues and circumstances surrounding you that require your attention. This is a good time to assess and calibrate all intentions to preserve balance.

Goal: Clean up any messes within your universe that can throw you out of balance.

Light: As one who takes responsibility for how they live in the world, you can enjoy the grace and creativity that surrounds you. Life is sweet and orderly.

Shadow: Chaos seems to reign and has its roots in your thought process. Take some time to review recent actions and decisions; then, if required, take right action to rectify a misdeed or misunderstanding.

History: We suspect that although the Maya were a people of rules and regulations, the real law was the law of the universe. Other than keeping a certain status quo amongst their population, their highest law was universal law, or the observable movements of the planets, and how that affected them. As Charles Phillips, *Aztec and Maya,* states:

> The Maya did not accept that bad things could happen by accident, for they viewed every event as the fulfillment of patterns that could be read in the stars and perhaps in the past, and which were set in motion by the gods.

When we think of law, we migrate to universal law, and for the purpose of this road map, it is that which we honor. It is as simple as physics: What goes up, must come down; or for every action there is an opposite and equal reaction. Or one can go back to folk wisdom and remember that what we sow, we reap.

If this card conjures images of retribution for misdeeds, preempt that with an understanding that we can avoid a great deal of grief by developing a conscious awareness of how we interact with and move through the world.

If you have drawn this card, it is cautioning that your actions are going to cause reactions. It could be that you are already in the process of renegotiating some misunderstanding with truth, or repaying a debt long overdue. It serves to remind us that we are part of a greater whole and our actions affect the universe. Consider every comment and thought before you commit yourself to action. Strive for fairness, harmony, and truth in all things. This card could also indicate that there are contracts or legal matters on the horizon.

8 Adjustment
LAW GIVER

9 Fortune
MAIZE GOD

Key: Wealth.

Inspiration: If you are reading this or hearing someone else interpret it, consider the advantages of hearing and sight. If you are interpreting this card for yourself, be thankful for a functioning brain. The idea of wealth is far beyond the concept of man-made currency.

Energetic: The appearance of this card in a reading indicates wealth. You may be about to realize the fruition of an investment or a gift that is coming to you. Without trying to describe how this wealth would look, it will bring a smile. It could be good results from a recent check-up, reassuring you of good health or an unexpected job offer in an area of interest that would satisfy you. It could be a fine meal or extra cash.

Goal: To be able to see the myriad number of ways we are wealthy.

Light: This card in a reading indicates a richness coming to you that will lighten your heart and substantiate your standing in the material world. It would indicate that life will be a little easier with some unexpected help.

Shadow: If this card appears in a poorly dignified place, you may be cultivating a poverty mentality that will only breed more poverty. It is time for you to look at how much you do have and celebrate-so that the energy that surrounds you can nurture more wealth.

History: In this card, the Earth is represented as a turtle shell. Notice the split in the center of the card, where you will see the Corn God and the emergence of the Na goddess with a burning torch at the top of the skull. At the openings on either side of the turtle shell you will see a water lily toad and Pax god emerge.[25]

The Corn God is flanked by the Headband Gods, who have been associated with the Hero Twins who represent the sun and the moon. The Headband Gods are positioned at the opposite ends of the "world," just as in nature; the sun is rising and the full moon is setting. The Jaguar Headband God is tipping over a jar of water, the same scene from many other depictions of rain gods dispersing rain.[26]

We have used the Maize God as their presentation of "Fortune" because Corn was the most important economic factor in the Mayan economy.[27] One could possess too much gold to carry, or command the greatest army, but nothing could be sustained without corn.

The corn God and his wife were also heavily associated with divination.[28] The Maya have a long history of relying on divination to guide them in their daily lives.

This card in a reading would be an indication to review your concept of wealth. Instead of contemplating what kind of car you are driving and how much your house is worth, one should be showing gratitude for sustenance at the most fundamental level. Will it take a polar shift for us to be thankful for the gifts of night and day, rain, sun, and Earth, and her produce? Will we enter a time when we will be reminded once again, how precious it is to have a jar of corn kernels to plant in the spring?

9 Fortune
MAIZE GOD

10 Lust
TLAZOLTEOTL

Key: Greed.

Inspiration: As we contemplate this card, we celebrate our diverse and creative ways of embracing life. A lust for learning and expansion are needed to meet this time of change; it is a sacred, primordial drive. We must, however, be discerning about our appetites and not indulge in the things that will sour our experience of what life has to give.

Energetic: When this card appears in a reading it is a warning. Perhaps the issue you are bringing to the cards is one of wanting what is not good for you. It could be that the relationship, either to the cosmos or to another person, is born of greed or the longing for excess which can create imbalance.

We can exhibit greed in many ways, even in spirituality. Wanting to know too much sometimes can be the desire for an unhealthy and destructive kind of power. Longing for a sexual partner that is not able to meet you where you are, can sometimes bring more pain and destruction than pleasure. Be careful of what you ask for.

Goal: The goal of this card is not only to recognize the hunger for power and greed within ourselves, but to transform that energy with love and compassion. Tlazolteotl is the eater of sins because she has learned from her own unbridled passions and is not afraid to traverse that world and eat the sins of mankind. It is through compassion, not passion, that she heals the errors of greed and lust.

Light: Vital energy, raw power, and earth-force strength of will.

Shadow: This can signify the desire to possess more than we are able to handle. This card also speaks of a longing for external sources of acceptance and acknowledgement rather than developing self love. The pleasure generated by greed and lust are perhaps some of the most dangerous illusions we entertain.

History: Tlazolteotl (Tlaz-ol-TEE-otl), the goddess of filth, excrement, and lust is a temptress, a sin-eater, and associated with penitential rites.[29]

In Aztec mythology, she used her sexual power to undo pious men. It is said that when the religious man would attempt to win favor, by surviving in the wilderness and only focus on their demanding religious observance, she would come. The goddess would sing to the man and plead for him to come to her. She would sing sweet songs from the brothels of Tenochtitlan, and moan sweetly. When that failed to draw his attention from his ritual, she would then dress beautifully and seductively and come to him. She would tell him that she only desired conversation and longed to learn from him. Like a sweet, gentle breeze, in the sun-baked dessert, the seductress would disarm the piety of the pilgrim and lure him into lust.[30]

Yaotl (enemy) would then appear beside the pilgrim and turn him into a scorpion. Afterward, the enemy would then bring the man's wife and turn her into a scorpion, where the man and wife would live under a rock and produce generations of scorpions.[31]

The other side of Tlazolteotl is that of penitent, she is also painted in the codices riding a snake and a broomstick with which she sweeps away the sins of the sorrowful.[32] She is petitioned to eat the sins of the many that disappear into the labyrinth of lust and greed. Sinners make offerings to her and revere her for her healing powers around sins of sexuality and greed.

For our purposes, Tlazolteotl is a sacrificial lamb. She has endured the hideous lessons of greed and lust so that she can traverse the darkness for those who wander from the spiritual path. She eats the sins of the pilgrims whose life has been defiled by lust.

10 Lust
TLAZOLTEOTL

II Hanged Man
SEVEN MACAW

Key: Evolution.

Inspiration: Create mental and spiritual space for a new world view. Allow yourself to imagine unity, peace, and a new era of personal responsibility that promotes you to position of co-creator with the Infinite. This could be the best "re-union" you've ever experienced.

Energetic: For the purpose of attempting to describe the paradigm shift, Seven Macaw is perhaps the most important card in the deck. He was an outdated guide for transformation, because of his inability to overcome the precessional movement of Planet Earth and remain the focal point in the heavens.

That is also true of our beliefs during these changing times. Duality, the concept of "us and them," the Cartesian idea that everything that exists within its own little box, no longer serves us. We simply can't continue to use fossil fuels without impacting our environment and depleting the "life blood" of Grandmother Earth.

It does not serve us to spend our energy fearing and resenting the circumstances that surround us. It is a time to find the divinity within, and re-create our world with a new understanding.

Goal: It is time to recognize the sacredness in all things; and realize that we are a critical part of a greater whole. It is time to stop living and acting as though we are the center of the universe and understand that we are no less than the stars and no greater than the corn that sustains us.

Light: As the polar caps are melting and the Earth's magnetosphere is changing, we too are shifting. Is it good or bad? It is all according to a plan that we are too limited to question. The enlightened approach is to be curious and grateful that we are witness and participants to a force far beyond our comprehension. We are in the midst of evolution on a physical and spiritual level that is unparalleled in human history. What could be more exciting! If this card shows in a beneficial position, it is an indication that you are, in thought and deed, doing the internal work necessary to accommodate a new perspective for the changes we are experiencing.

Shadow: To try to hold on to old belief systems will not only constipate you, it could kill you. If your predominate response to current events is one of dread, try to remember that, like flowers and trees, the process only gets more beautiful and multidimensional.

History: The *Popol Vuh* describes Vucub-Caquix (vo KOB ka KWISH) as Seven Macaw, the bird demon who pretended to be the sun and the moon of the twilight world, in between the former creation and the present one. The false sun-moon, Seven Macaw, was shot out of his tree, while eating a meal, by Hunahpu, one of the Maya Hero Twins. Together, the Hero Twins became the present-day true sun and true moon.[33]

Perhaps the imagery of Seven Macaw is more easily understood, when one realizes that the Maya used Seven Macaw to refer to the seven stars in the Big Dipper. His wife, Chimalmat, is the Little Dipper. They perceived the handle of the Big Dipper as the long, brightly colored tail feathers of the mystical parrot.[34]

Seven Macaw, the cosmic bird that thought he was the sun, was a gorgeous bird, who brightened a dark world with his majesty. His eyes were bright silver and jade, his teeth blue with beautiful stones and his plumage bright and rich.[35]

Enchantment with the "heavenly bird" changed in time, because the Ancients used the pole star at the most northerly part of the big dipper as their navigational guide. With the precession of the Earth, (remember, that is a term identifying the wobble of the Earth, rather than its trajectory through the universe), the pole star shifted and began to disappear into the northern horizon. By doing this, Seven Macaw lost his value in calculating time and movement through the cosmos. This change in the heavenly landscape was the basis for the mythology of Seven Macaw, a false god.[36]

11 Hanged Man
SEVEN MACAW

12 Death
TZITZIMITL

Key: Renewal.

Inspiration: Death is a transformation; we die and resurrect every day. Whether we endure the death of a relationship, the end of a career; or the setting of the sun signaling the death of a day we will never see again, death is part of living. Rather than fear this idea, rejoice in the possibility of growth and renewal. Fear nothing.

Energetic: If Tzitzimitl appears in your reading, she could be warning you of a change in attitude or about the death of a situation or an idea that holds you back. As we die to our old ways, new ideas replace the old and challenge us to think, move, and act in a different way. Change rarely takes us backwards or diminishes us. It is through the discomfort of change and renewal that we learn our mortal lessons and sharpen our soulful instincts for compassion and love.

Goal: To let the ideas that reduce us to fear and resentment die. We have an opportunity, with this card in our reading, to reassess our thoughts and relationships and let go of what does not serve a higher level of consciousness.

Light: This card in a beneficial placement in your reading would be to honor work you have done to change a poor perception to a clearer view and understanding of your reality. It is a card heralding transformation. Isn't that what this experience is all about?

Shadow: To miss an opportunity for greater understanding and growth is perhaps the most frightening death we can experience. If this card is in a negative position, your perceptions of your reality are diminishing you.

History: Tzitzimitl (tsee tsee MEETL) is an Aztec deity associated with stars. There are four of these female deities that were worshipped by midwives and parturient women.[37] They are depicted as skeletal figures wearing skirts with skull and cross bone designs. With a necklace of eyes and paper flags in their hair, they were a frightening sight.

Tzitzimitl is also associated with fertility and the stars that can be seen around the sun during a solar eclipse. Because of the chaotic nature of eclipses, the Tzitzimime were thought to be attacking the sun and, therefore, would come to Earth to devour human beings.[38]

The Tzitzimime were considered the protectors of the feminine, the progenitresses of mankind. These deities were considered powerful and dangerous. They were acknowledged especially during periods of cosmic instability or during the five unlucky days of the Aztec year count. They were also a part of the New Fire Ceremony, which marks the beginning of a new calendar round. These periods were times associated with fear and change; and the belief that without the proper offerings and observances, the sun would no longer rise, leaving the world in total darkness.[39]

For our purposes, Tzitzimitl characterizes the idea of death because of her influence on fertility and birth. Death is a birth, of sorts, into a new dimension of being. Who is not to say that we are not in the land of the dead, here on Earth, and that full life would not be more possible without all of the requirements and constraints of physical existence?

This card represents for us, a reminder to face the daily deaths of this life with an idea of renewal and regeneration.

12 Death
TZITZIMITL

13 Vision
VISION SERPENT

Key: Look Within.

Inspiration: It is beneficial to create a space and time for prayer or meditation, each day. Our own personal vision serpent is always available to offer perspective and guidance. Whether we are in need of immediate answers or not, it is a great way to stay in tune with what is true for us at any given moment.

Energetic: Oftentimes, we need to move out of the mundane in order to see a situation or person more clearly. The Maya did it through ritual bloodletting; contemporary Native Americans seek answers by sitting on a hill and fasting. Take about thirty minutes a day, of meditation or prayer, to connect with your endless potential.

Goal: It is ideal to carve a little time out of each day, to listen to the innate wisdom available to each of us. Remember, Spirit informs matter. We have but to develop our inner vision and hearing to know that we are guided by the infinite.

Light: In a good position, the Vision Serpent is reminding you that you already have the answer within yourself. Take a break from the confusion and chaos, pray and be prepared to listen.

Shadow: It is so easy to be lost in a sea of other people's concerns and emotions. Often, the problems that loom on our horizon are not even our own. If this card appears, it is time to pull away, breath, contemplate, and reorient yourself to what is yours to do and what is not yours to do. It is time to conjure your own Vision Serpent for guidance.

History: This image from Yaxchilan, (Chiapas, Mexico), Lintel 25, depicts the pinnacle of a blood sacrifice. Lady Xoc, principal consort and wife, of King Itzamna Balham III, is asking for a vision for her husband as he prepares for ascension to the throne.[40]

Often times a stingray spine would pierce the tongue of the seeker, releasing blood, which was soaked into papers made of bark. Her blood sacrifice, is placed in a bowl, where the bark paper which has absorbed the blood is burned, causing a column of smoke to rise. The Vision Serpent then appears in the smoke column and allows the deities, ancestors, or deceased warriors to communicate with the seeker. In this way, the ancestors and gods were invited to participate in any political or religious event.[41]

Although many have tried to explain the phenomenon of bloodletting, the consensus is that the loss of blood causes "the brain to release an abundance of natural endorphins, which are chemically related to opiates. As the body goes into shock, a visual or auditory hallucination can occur."[42]

In royal Maya courts, women were allowed to participate in political and religious roles, unlike other Mesoamerican cultures. It was Lady Xoc who commissioned the lintels during the reign of her husband.[43]

For our purposes, the Vision card is an invitation or suggestion to seek a vision for the question at hand. It does not have to hurt and you do not have to bleed. Take a long walk or meditate on your concerns and "see" if you can hear the voice of your ancestors. Allow your inner vision to become active.

13 Vision
VISION SERPENT

14 Devil
EARTH MONSTER

Key: Destruction, playfulness.

Inspiration: When the Earth Monster card appears in a reading, either in a beneficial or negative light, it is time to review what it is you want and what you really need. It is a warning to assess where you are, who you are, and who you desire to be.

Energetic: The Earth Monster card represents the relentless desire for power and greed for earthly possessions. It can also represent the deep darkness we enter into, to realize the value of light.

Goal: When this card appears in a reading, it is an indication to review and check your desires or motives for interaction with the world. The practice of greed can carry a huge price, namely your freedom, and baggage you may not want to carry. Take the warning and travel light.

Light: In a good position, the Earth Monster might indicate an adventure and a period of playfulness.

Shadow: In a poorly dignified position, this card could indicate delusion and corruption in your actions or thought process. You may be acting out of an obsession or compulsion rather than choosing a right course of action. It is a warning to beware of the territory you are entering, physically, mentally or spiritually. The cost for admission could be your soul.

History: This replica of the Earth Monster is usually found on the cylindrical base of the sky emblem. The two emblems together are perhaps the most important images in Aztec art, depicting the dualistic nature of reality. The sun disk represents the rational order of time, the light of day; as opposed to the chaotic nature of darkness, that of unformed matter and unmeasured time.[44]

We use the Earth Monster card as the archetype for the Devil card because it is a beast with head thrown back, hair full of poison insects and skulls with teeth like sacrificial knives.[45] It represents chaos, darkness, confusion, and instability.

The Earth Monster can bring about an unbridled greed and lust for power over the physical world. It carries a destructive energy that can reverse the natural flow of energy; and can be considered a "half truth." The most dangerous lie that is told is the one that has a face of truth; and beneath the illusion is error.

In a benign position, the Earth Monster card can indicate a devilish playfulness or the desire to cut loose from ties that hinder one's development. It is rare that we grow or come to understand light and shadow from only a righteous perspective. It is through our unbridled desire and appetite that we learn the value of moderation and simplicity. Greed can teach us that traveling light, without the burden of too many possessions and entanglements can be the best of all possibilities. Greed and possession are heavy burdens and can induce unconsciousness within our naturally curious and adventurous souls. Unless we have experienced the heaviness of our greed or desire, how can we know how wonderful it is to be unencumbered?

14 Devil
EARTH MONSTER

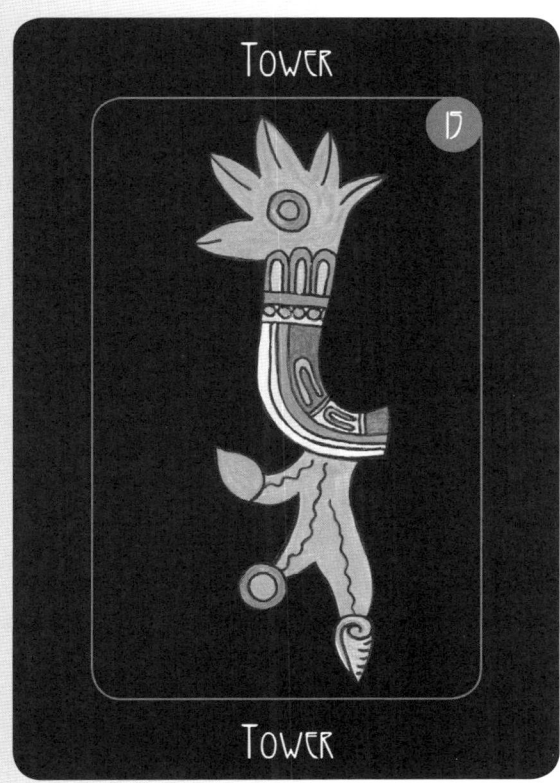

15 Tower
FIRE/WATER/STREAM

Key: Chaos, opportunity.

Inspiration: When this card shows itself to you, it is to remind you that one cannot control anything. There are no muscles you can flex in the face of drought or famine; but you can teach yourself how to conserve water, how to grow a garden, and how to make something valuable out of anything. This card is calling you to be flexible and aware that potential and possibility are more available in chaos than at any other time. Think of remodeling a house, how hard is it to tear down a structure already in place and change it? It is much easier to raze an old building and start fresh instead of patching and remodeling.

Energetic: The energy of this card is chaos. It could be drawing attention to chaotic thinking, a messy environment or a restructuring of your life. It is an indicator that this is not a time of "business as usual" for you. It is important not to engage the chaos, but rather observe how and where it is manifesting in your life.

Goal: Like a tidal wave, life circumstances can sweep us up and carry us to unforeseen places. We never have to be victims of circumstance; when possible, grab a board and surf the wave with the intention of enjoying the ride. Never be afraid of unforeseen or unplanned circumstances. This is one way Creator gets our attention and helps us remember why we are here.

Light: It would be hard to convince anyone that chaos is a good thing or to inspire a longing for such; but it is often the energetic that will pull us out of a deep well of immobility and stagnation. If this card comes up in a beneficial place in your spread, consider that the circumstances that are brewing around you are to insure your soul's expansion and agility. These will be beneficial trials that will strengthen you.

Shadow: In a poorly dignified position, it could indicate that your lack of awareness and sheer laziness are creating a chaotic life. This is not a good circumstance because it is through resignation that you can create your own victimhood. Stay awake, be alert, and make choices that will strengthen your being.

History: The Fire/Water/Stream is an emblem, usually attached to another glyph or image. The intertwined fire-water symbol is a stream of water as a band with segmented sections and a flame design taken from the fire serpent.[46]

The visual can be related to the concept "divine liquid fire," or it can represent the idea of war or severe drought caused by the sun's unrelenting rays. It can also be seen as pestilence.[47] It is included in Aztec artwork as something coming out of the mouth of a figure predicting or describing the experience of chaos.

The image of water and fire together is a suggestion that both elements are in contrast and associated with one another. This image can suggest, through the use of fire and water, that together, the dynamic can initiate and sustain fertility and/or destruction of life. The image of rushing water reminds us of our impermanence and the transient nature of life.

We use this image as the Tower card because of the chaos that can come out of nowhere and affect our lives in unforeseen ways. It is a hazard of living, yet, it is from these chaotic circumstances that we often are led to our ultimate destiny. Consider J. K. Rowling and her books about Harry Potter. She was on welfare and writing at local coffee shops. Harry Potter would not have found such a powerful voice in too much comfort or security.

If this card comes up in a reading, it would definitely alert you to a potential for unforeseen chaos, but it could be something as grand as a disturbance that would rouse you from a deep sleep and spur you into an action that would change your world for the better. Instead of causing a breakdown, it could create a breakthrough.

15 Tower
FIRE/WATER/STREAM

16 Star
LAMAT

Key: As you wish.

Inspiration: Just as a star illuminates darkness, it is the longing and desire to create that keeps us vital and alive. Our dreams are not mere illusions, but a light in the void that can lead us back to Source. To manifest your dream, is to offer yourself to the world.

Energetic: The Star card is about optimism, enthusiasm, destiny, and hope. It represents an innocence of belief, that anything is possible. It inspires us to create instead of observe. If this card is appearing in your spread, you are being challenged to find your dream; visualize it and believe it is possible.

Goal: Dare to dream, to create, and to believe.

Light: If this card is in a beneficial place, trust your vision and let your dream manifest. Remember that Spirit informs matter.

Shadow: If the Star card shows in a negative place, you are dealing with an illusion—an untruth. It is time to go back to the drawing board and revisit what you thought you wanted. It could be that your dream is destructive and a roadblock to your soul's evolution.

History: The Maya name for Venus is Lamat (la-MAHT).[48] It is and was perhaps for the Ancients, the most important celestial body, other than the sun and moon. For our purposes, Venus as the morning star is our symbol for the Star card in other decks.

In Mesoamerican mythology, astronomical events are inseparable from their creation myths. Each story is a lyrical description of what was happening in the heavens. Each movement of the celestial bodies carried an energetic that had great implications regarding what was happening in the Middleworld or the Earth plane. This is not unlike present-day astrology.

To the Maya, Venus was related to the Hero Twins, war, and the planting season. In its complex journey through our galaxy, Venus repeats its orbit every eight years and was an important touch stone for the prediction of wars, the success or failure of crops, and rain.[49]

Some of the Mayan texts refer to Venus as Quetzalcoatl and attribute some of the maligning influences of war and aggression to this star.

The myth of Quetzalcoatl "closely parallels the Venus cycle."[50] In the Aztec tradition, Quetzalcoatl was humiliated by the followers of Tezcatlipoca and "he sacrificed himself on a funeral pyre and his soul rose from his body as Venus,"[51] the star of dawn. In this form he was considered an "enemy of the sun."[52]

The Star card represents optimism and hope. It is "as you wish" with this card. We know that before any dreams can take on a physical reality, there must be the dream. The Star card is about creating your reality. If you think you can do it, you can. If you doubt, forget about it.

16 Star
LAMAT

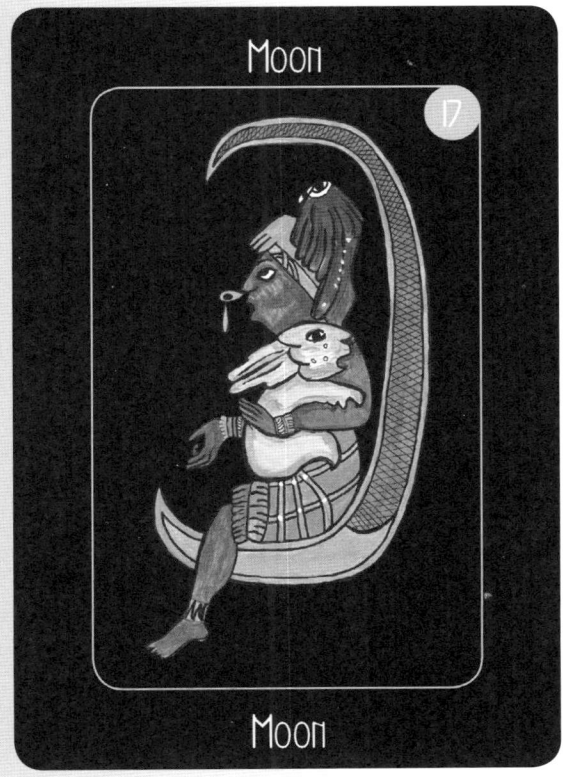

17 Moon
IX CHEL

Key: Embracing the shadow.

Inspiration: As the moon changes its form each night and disappears to the other side of the world to reemerge again as a crescent moon, our flight into the subconscious or "Underworld" is a rebirth. This is a journey back and forth, through the veil of life and death. We come back with a deeper understanding of what it is to be human—to change and grow, to suffer and recover. In terms of relationship, it is a signal of fantasy and changeability that indicates an unstable foundation for a long-lasting partnership.

Energetic: It is generally considered that the Moon card represents our deepest unidentified desires and fears. It relates to the idea of lunacy and to the concept of the 28-day orbital cycle of the moon as it relates to Earth.

Goal: The Moon card can affirm that we are intimate with self, that we acknowledge what is real and what is fantasy. It can be a card that confirms that our soul is integrated with our outward appearance. Our existence and purpose are aligned.

Light: This card in a beneficial placement could indicate that we have done the work necessary to allow our intuitive instincts to guide us. It could reflect our ability to descend into the Underworld of our existence with confidence and that we have the skills and knowledge to come back with greater understanding.

Shadow: In a poor placement, the Moon card can indicate delusion, drug abuse, fear, and a sojourn in to the "dark night of the soul" with no tools or skills to re-emerge.

History: We have used the Maya moon goddess, Ix Chel (Esh CHEL) as the Moon card because she represents birth, medicine, and rain. Her feast day is celebrated by physicians and shamans[53], accentuating the idea that the moon is the bridge between the conscious and unconscious mind.

According to Mesoamerican scholar Karl Taube, Ix Chel is not a beautiful young woman, but an old crone who is the patron of midwives. She is also the Great Mother of all birthing processes, both mythological and biological.

Not only were the city states of the ancients aligned with the heavens, anthropologists found among the Chorti and Yucatec Maya, homes which had their roofs designed with crossbeams to depict the four directions. The top joint symbolized the birth cleft, or dark rift of the Milky Way.

For childbirth, a rope would be hung from the top joint and would be used as a "birthing rope." The expectant mother would not only stabilize herself during a delivery this way, but would be re-enacting the creation story of the cosmos.[54]

This link between the cosmos and a birthing mother helps us to understand the sky as cosmic mother and the dark rift as the birth cleft. The Xibalba is the mythic birth canal or the Cosmic Womb according to the Tzotzil Maya.[55]

In present-day Mesoamerica, there are still believers who journey to Cozumel and Isla Mujeres, to pay tribute to the goddess Ix Chel and to petition her for help in matters of marriage, childbirth, and issues that face aging women.

IxChelis also associated with the waning moon or the phase of womanhood where the jar of life-giving fluid is being emptied, like the rain from the heavens, childbirth, or aging .In this facet, the moon is referred to as "grandmother."

17 Moon
IX CHEL

18 Sun
QUETZALCOATL

Key: Reconciliation.

Inspiration: The sun signifies a celebration of life, a confident interaction with our surroundings and a self confidence that can allow the unfolding of hidden potential. It can indicate an outgoing, warm personality or alliance in relationship or business.

Energetic: For our purposes, the Sun card signifies the source of all that is holy. The sun gives light without reservation or negotiation, but it can burn and scorch if not respected.

Goal: As we grow and expand, we allow light into the deepest cracks of our being. The Sun card indicates a movement towards reconciliation with our shadow side and bids us to walk, without excuse or apology, into the light of day.

Light: When the Sun card appears in your spread, it can indicate an open, warm, and nurturing relationship with your world and the cosmos. It is a card of unlimited optimism. Just as the sun channels light from the cosmos to our Mother

Earth, we can transmit that limitless energy into any situation. It could refer to a creative, productive, and joyful situation in romance or business.

Shadow: In a poorly dignified position, the Sun card could indicate delusions of grandeur and a searing, critical nature. Self satisfaction is often born of a very limited perspective or extreme tunnel vision.

History: For the Sun card, we have used the image of Quetzalcoatl (ket sahl KO ahtl) dragging the sun's rays across the heavens from the Underworld, to nourish all of life in the Middleworld.

The sky was sacred to the Mesoamericans. Many of their rituals were to insure the sun's re-emergence from the Underworld, each day.

Some Maya traditions define the four directions by the movement of the sun:[56]

> The East is where the "sun emerges."
> The West is the place where the "sun exits."
> The North is the place of the sun's zenith at noon.
> The South represents the darkest hour, the sun's nadir, when the sun fights for its life against the Lords of Darkness in the Underworld.

As explained by Esther Pasztory, in *Aztec Art*:

> The two basic metaphors for transformation in ancient Mesoamerica were sexuality and death, because both were seen to result in the creation of life. The sexual metaphor was used to explain the renewal of nature... The sun god was believed to descend into the Earth at the end of the dry season and to mate with the Earth goddess, who then gave birth to the maize and other plants that grow in the rainy season. The sun god died in the sexual encounter, to be reborn in the form of maize. The Earth goddess died subsequently in the process of giving birth... Since nature was believed to be in a state of balance, no new life could be created without the death of the old.

Ometeotl and Omecihuatl, the Lord and Lady of Duality, are considered the personification of the sun god and goddess and thereby the creators of the universe. They represent the duality of nature; the male and female principal of the universe. While some scholars see the Lord and Lady of Duality as separate entities, such as the sun and the Earth; some see Ometeotl as one god embodying both principals.[57]

18 Sun
QUETZALCOATL

19 Stillness
WATER LILY

Key: Authenticity.

Inspiration: So often, we are striving to understand another person or situation and feel frustrated and flattened by that effort. There is no personal act more powerful than to find one's center and move from there.

Energetic: Out of stillness comes quietude, flexibility, and adaptability. The water lily plant lives in and out of the water, adapting to the watery environment below, and drawing the nourishing rays of the sun from above. It endures the relentless heat and the unseen currents below. This beautiful flower withstands these powerful forces of nature and is still able to offer a sweet and sensual beauty to the world.

Goal: Allow yourself a posture of quietude and stillness. Give yourself permission to retreat from the noise that surrounds you and find the essence of your being. This is your true strength and endurance.

Light: When this card comes up in a reading, it suggests that you stop paying attention and homage to the blustery noise that surrounds you—whether it is social interaction, television or just too much activity. Stillness will restore your vital energy and grant you an opportunity to become intimate with yourself once again. In this state, nothing can disturb you.

Shadow: If this card comes up in a poorly dignified position, say next to a relationship card, it would suggest holding silence for awhile. Listen instead of talk.

History: On many of the Maya vases and other art objects, we find the water lily symbol used by itself or in concert with other symbols. The water lily grows itself in the dark stillness of a pond or lake before it emerges, intact, to appear on the surface in all its glory.

The water lily may have served as a symbol for the convergence of the Underworld and Overworld. It appears to represent a microcosmic symbol of Earth. Many of the renderings of the water lily flower portray fish nibbling on the plant from below the surface, and birds feeding on the flower from above the surface. Its veined leaves, to some, suggest yet another replica of the lines on a turtle shell, which among the Maya, the turtle represents the "circular Earth floating upon the sea."[58]

The two gods most associated with the water lily are the Underworld's Water Lily Jaguar and the Water Lily Serpent, which symbolize "the surface of still water."[59] This flower adorns temples, headdresses of kings, and pottery in the ancient artifacts of the Maya, celebrating a profuse and enduring presence in the Maya lowlands of Mesoamerica.

For our purposes, this card reminds us to be still and aware. Chaos and confusion may surround you, but when you are able to still yourself and find your peace, it will not confound nor deter your soul's purpose.

19 Stillness
WATER LILY

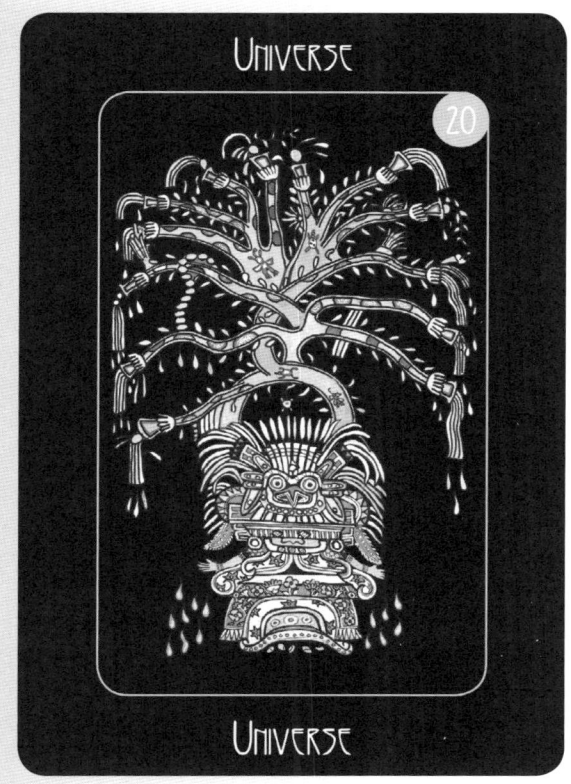

20 Universe
TEOTIHUACÁN SPIDER WOMAN

Key: Unity.

Inspiration: Getting back in harmony with the Creator. Merging with the balance of the cosmos and realigning with your spiritual purpose.

Energetic: The Universe card is a call to remember that we are timeless, limitless beings living in the illusion of time and space. We cannot fathom the size of our own universe, much less the countless other universes traversing the sea of the void. We are part of this grand creation and resonate with the infinite. It is only our thought constructs that keep us imprisoned in small identities and limited possibilities.

Goal: Remember who you are, no different than the sun or moon or stars. We exist in the mind of Creator.

Light: When this card shows up in a reading, it is a reassurance that you are in touch with your vast potential. Dare to dream and create what you came to create. Trust your instincts—you are on track.

Shadow: When this card shows up in a poorly dignified position, it could be a warning that you are deluding yourself and living an illusion. It's time to get honest about who you are and what you want to be. This can take work; prepare to spend time contemplating the vastness of the universe—you are home. All is well.

History: We have chosen the Teotihuacán (tay oh TEE wah kahn) Spider Woman as the traditional Universe card. Very little is known about this image.

Anthropologists were able to identify the image, found amongst some of the most beautiful mural, still intact, in Teotihuacán. "Pasztory concluded that the figures represented a vegetation and fertility goddess that was a predecessor of the much later Aztec goddess Xochiquetzal. In 1983, Karl Taube named this goddess image the 'Teotihuacan Spider Woman.'"[60]

As the artwork suggests, Spider Woman wove the universe into existence, starting with the Cosmic Tree, which unites the Overworlds, the Underworlds, and the Middleworld (Earth plane). As she sang and wove, Spider Woman incorporated life into Earth's children and taught them how to weave and make pottery. She is the grandmother of humanity and of the cosmos.

If we think about an ordinary spider web, we can appreciate the idea of the Teotihuacán Spider Woman in a more modern sense, as she weaves the matrix of existence and allows us to traverse the universe by traveling the energetic bio-magnetic web that she put into place. We are just beginning to understand the power of the concept, as we investigate interdimensional realities and develop our own abilities to perceive past, present, and future in the eternal and ever present moment.

If we contemplate the grid of communication that exists globally, we can appreciate how little we know about this invisible web or matrix that we are a part of. The information is not new; the Mayans were using this grid thousands of years ago to travel back and forth in time to make the predictions that we are so interested in today. They were aware of and working with non-local reality and quantum physics energetic concepts since before 3100 B.C.E.[61] The Universe card suggests wholeness and unity, a return to source. It suggests an overview of circumstance that gives every fragment of existence a new meaning as we begin to see ourselves and our experiences within a larger framework.

As we complete a 26,000 year cycle[62] and observe the end of the 9th and final Underworld,[63] we can only surmise that we are entering another golden age of enlightenment.

20 Universe
TEOTIHUACÁN
SPIDER WOMAN

21 Self Love
XOCHIQUETZAL

Key: Respect.

Inspiration: We cannot truly appreciate nor honor the sanctity or beauty of life without respecting and loving ourselves. Trying to own beauty is like looking for the pot of gold at the end of the rainbow. You can chase the color-band all you want, but as you get too close, it disappears. Look inside for that rainbow, it starts and ends there.

Energetic: If this card appears in your reading, it is a reminder to appreciate the beauty of the world but not try to own or manhandle it. You can appreciate what it is, without involving yourself. To find the true beauty that resides in you, it can sometimes only come with loss or disappointment.

Goal: To walk in beauty, think in beauty, and act in beauty.

Light: The beneficial side of this card is that it reminds us that we are part of a magnificent creation; we are no less stunning than the beautiful trees and stars and oceans. We do not have to rob beauty from anyone or anything else to possess the same qualities.

Shadow: If this card appears in a negative position, it would suggest that you are failing to see your own unique beauty and desirability.

History: Xochiquetzal (Sho-shee-KAY-tzall) was a beautiful Aztec goddess maiden living in the high mountain air of Tamoanchan, a blessed place at the level of the Thirteen Heavens. Although it was an earthly garden, only gods and goddesses lived there.

In the midst of the lovely garden, hidden near the holy peak of the mythical mountain in the south, the land of Huitzilopochtli was a stunningly beautiful cosmic tree. Xochiquetzal, the beautiful goddess maiden, so gifted in weaving and pottery, was happy there and loved the mountain, garden, and tree. She was surrounded with such beauty and fragrance from the blossoms and fruit of the cosmic tree that she couldn't help but be blissful.

Creator god Ometeotl had warned Xochiquetzal, not to touch the tree or eat its fruit. It was forbidden!

One spring day, Xochi watched the birds land on the branches and partake of the fruits. She was ecstatic with the warm breezes and beauty of the garden. She could not contain herself and picked a fragrant blossom and put it in her hair and picked a piece of fruit to eat. No sooner had she bitten into the fruit when it fell from her hands. The tree split in half and left a blood stain on the ground where it had dropped.

Almost immediately, creator god Ometeotl came and banished her to the arid desert lowlands where she stayed for eternity. He was determined to uphold his supreme command, so he removed her to the barren lowlands with cracked earth and took her sight through "ever-flowing tears."[64] Xochiquetzal is the bringer of beauty and flowers; she adorns men and women alike with beauty, but cries, because she cannot see.

For our purposes, Xochiquetzal represents inner beauty and self love; her lesson was a brutal one, she lost her eyesight only to learn to see with her heart. She still spreads beauty wherever she goes, because it resides within her, not outside of her.

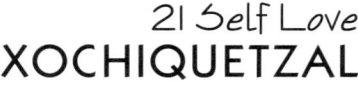

21 Self Love
XOCHIQUETZAL

Supernatural guardian, protector; Holy hand of Hunab K'u; walk with me, in grace and dignity, to serve Creator in all forms, all ways.

~Patricia A. Padilla
from *Secrets of Mayan Science/Religion*
Artwork by Patricia A. Padilla

Chapter 3

First Father

First Father, Emergence

The First Father card is a rendition of First Father (One Hunahpu) as inspired by Stela 11, group B of the Izapa monument groups. It is the highest spiritual card in the deck with no negative aspect. There is no use for a dualistic interpretation for this symbol, because it is the one artifact that suggests the end of the illusion of separation.

The outstretched hands of the First Father indicate the end of a "period-ending event."[1] This card suggests a rebirth, or a transition from Time to No Time, an end to dualities, and a reunion with Source.

According to Mayan researcher John Major Jenkins, when the frog's mouth is upright and open, its meaning is "rebirth."[2] The suggestion of this glyph is one of approaching the dark rift or center of the Milky Way, the birthing place of the stars, for our own rebirth and transformation.

Although there are many scholars with as many different interpretations, for our purposes, let it be understood that this card indicates an expansion and renewal that we don't have words for. It is a state of being, a conscious awareness of our relationship to the cosmos.

Although we have a new language emerging for ideas like non-local reality (coined by Albert Einstein in 1913), zero point (Bell's Theorem), and "holographic resonance,"[3] these are not new realities. It is we who are unfolding to the endless possibilities of creation. This is evolution. We have arrived and now are capable of creating the reality we prefer. If you pulled this card, consider that your world is opening in a new and remarkable way, allowing your universal essence to come forward. You have outgrown your physical identity and the constraints of limited thinking. There is no need to ask or worry about love, money, career, or direction, for you exist as the breath of Creator, inseparable from the creative force that holds us all in orbit.

First Father
EMERGENCE

Inspiration: You are already in a state of grace: you have the "keys to the kingdom." It is time for your mind to catch up.

As we evolve from the murky waters of the Piscean age into the crisp, clear air of Aquarius, we will be freed of the illusions and misconceptions of limitation. As we leave the Piscean age, ruled by the planet Neptune, it is as we have been submerged in the gloomy waters of misunderstanding and incarceration. We have actually believed and perpetuated those ideas of separation and limitation. This new age is characterized by freedom. We are beginning to experience freedom from the illusion that we are our body, or our story. This new age we are entering is an act of "re-remembering" that we are love incarnate, limited only by our own willful self deceptions.

Chapter 4

The Cycle of Days

Acceptance, 1 Day
Expression, 2 Day
Security, 3 Day
Leadership, 4 Day
Energetics, 5 Day
Instinct, 6 Day
Authenticity, 7 Day
Moderation, 8 Day
Persistence, 9 Day
Authority, 10 Day

Creativity, 11 Day
Emotions, 12 Day
Knowledgeable, 13 Day
Wisdom, 14 Day
Ambition, 15 Day
Overcome, 16 Day
Flexibility, 17 Day
Share, 18 Day
Curiosity, 19 Day
Simplicity, 20 Day

The Tzolkin 260-day calendar is the sacred calendar of the Maya. Within the 260-day period of the calendar, there are thirteen (13) twenty-day cycles called the Tricena. The thirteen cycles carry a different energy or frequency; but for our purposes, we will focus on the energetic of the twenty days.

The twenty-day signs are very specific spiritual energies that repeat and give each day its unique spiritual quality. Astrological correlations to the day signs have given the Maya a tool with which to identify the qualities a child is born with, and a directional signal with which to help the child grow to maturity. Each of us is born with the unique spiritual qualities and challenges that occurred in the cosmos at the time of our birth.

The thirteen Overworlds, nine Underworlds, in addition to the twenty Day signs, give us a wealth of information to consider as we encounter any individual or circumstance. It is like an intersection point that one can delineate in an effort to understand what energies are in action to form our earthly experience.

What differentiates the Maya method of time keeping from all others is the fixed, but repetitive, cycling of specific energies that describe birth, death, and rebirth. These reoccurring energies within the larger cycles of time define ritual activities of the Maya and lend an identifiable pattern to the movement of time for divination. Calleman states in his book, *The Mayan Calendar and the Transformation of Consciousness*:

> The timeline of the Mayan calendar, by contrast (to astrology, kabbalah, numerology, and Tarot as examples of divinatory tools), is unambiguously true and not of a hocus-pocus nature. Anyone with access to a standard encyclopedia can verify its validity from the facts of biological and historical evolution.

Each day sign is also associated with one of the four directions, which carries another energetic force. Scofield and Orr, *How to Practice Mayan Astrology,* created a table of concepts associated with each direction.[1] Listed below are a few of these concepts for each **Direction:**

East

Associated with initiation with the power of creativity.

North

Associated with separation with a power of materialization.

West

Associated with cooperation and carries the power of communication.

South

Associated with connection and carries the power of emotion.

Even though there are many layers to the energetics of the Day cards, these are enough to give the seeker a flavor of the forces they are experiencing.

ACCEPTANCE
1 Day

Energy: Initiating, protective.

Day Name: IMIX (ee-Mish).

Direction: East.

Symbol: Crocodile, the reptilian body of the planet.

Challenge: Learn self acceptance and become comfortable as an equal in social or familial situations. Watch out for domineering or territorial behaviors.

Solution: Learn to be independent and cooperative within your community and relationships. Learn to give from your essence not just your excess.

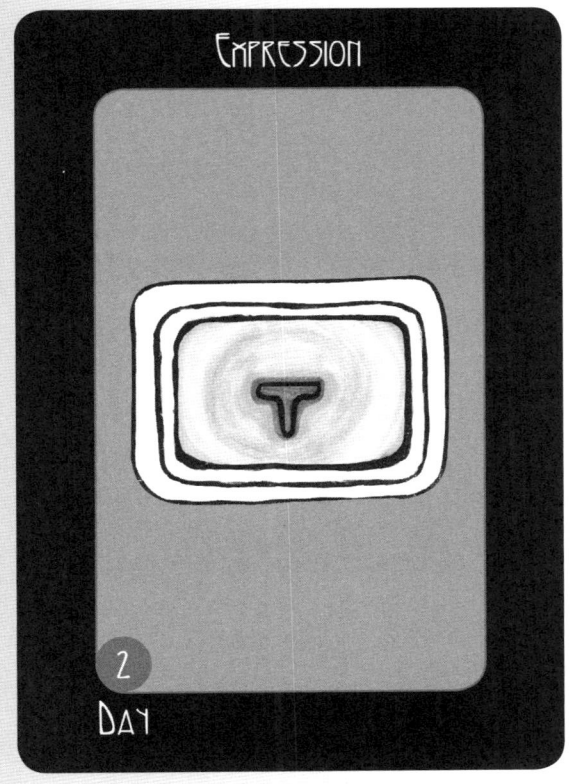

EXPRESSION
2 Day

Energy: Communications, spiritual, multi-faceted.

Day Name: IK (eek).

Direction: North.

Symbol: Wind, expression, air, breath, and life.

Challenge: Learn to accept responsibility and to be clear in communicating your wants, needs, and concerns.

Solution: Develop communication skills.

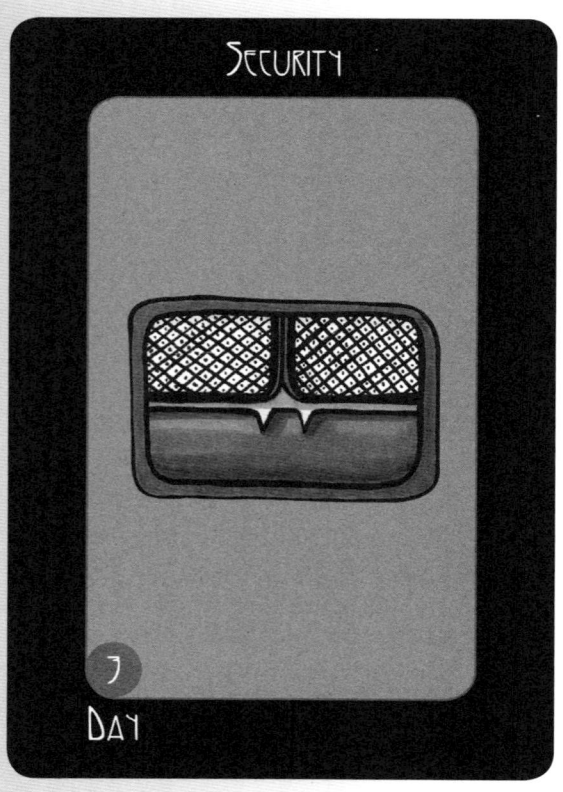

SECURITY
3 Day

Energy: Powerful, organized, home oriented.

Day Name: AKBAL (ak-Bal).

Direction: West.

Symbol: Darkness, realm of nocturnal jaguar-sun, the Night House.

Challenge: Rigid thinking, need for control, and difficulty in sharing.

Solution: Flexibility, flexibility, flexibility; and let go.

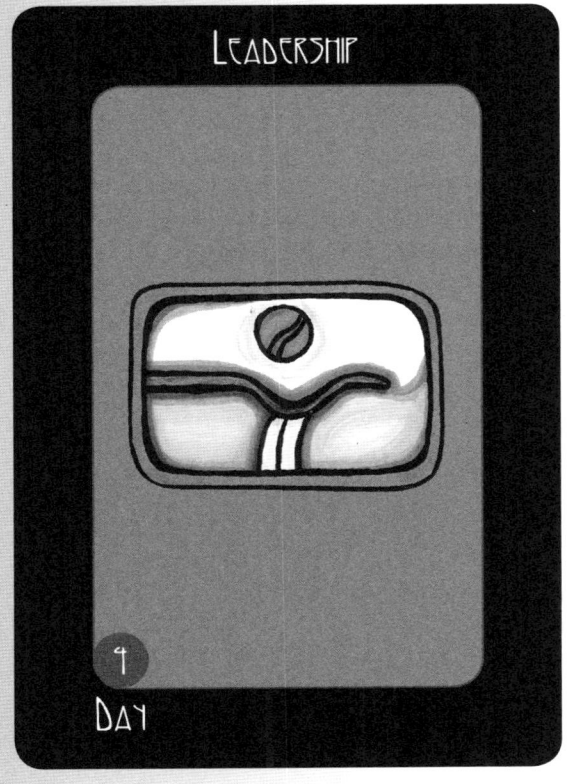

LEADERSHIP
4 Day

Energy: Active, dynamic, sexual, performance.

Day Name: KAN (kahn).

Direction: South.

Definition: Maize, abundance, ripeness.

Challenge: Strive for balance in all endeavors and develop a healthy self esteem.

Solution: Pay attention to details and stay open to possibilities.

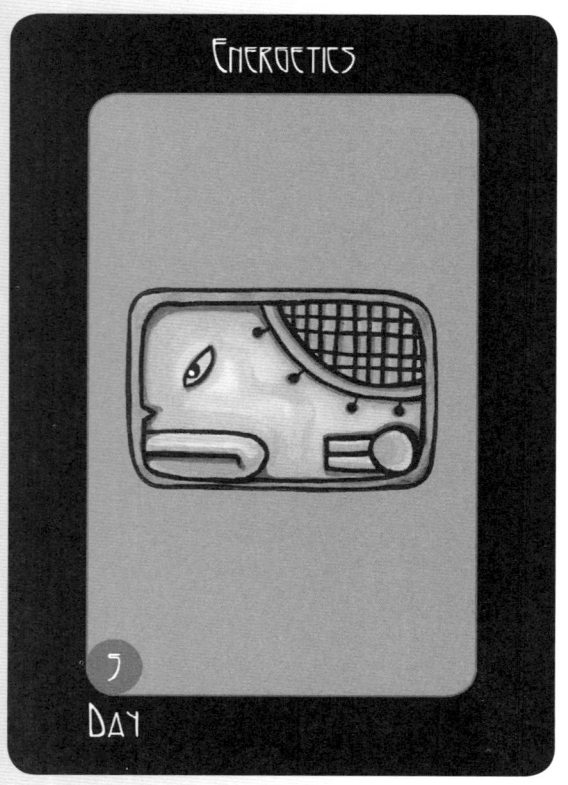

ENERGETICS
5 Day

Energy: Strong-willed, charismatic, and powerful.

Day Name: CHICCHAN (Chee-chan).

Direction: East.

Symbol: Snake, the celestial serpent.

Challenge: Strive to consciously transform your energy in everything you do for the benefit of all.

Solution: Develop a compassionate understanding of life, death, and living.

INSTINCT
6 Day

Energy: Security conscious, material realm, traditional.

Day Name: CIMI (kee-Mee).

Direction: North.

Symbol: Owl, death, sacrifice, preservation.

Challenge: Avoid being a victim, doormat, or martyr.

Solution: Make your efforts count in your relationships, community, and world. Build your "faith" muscles.

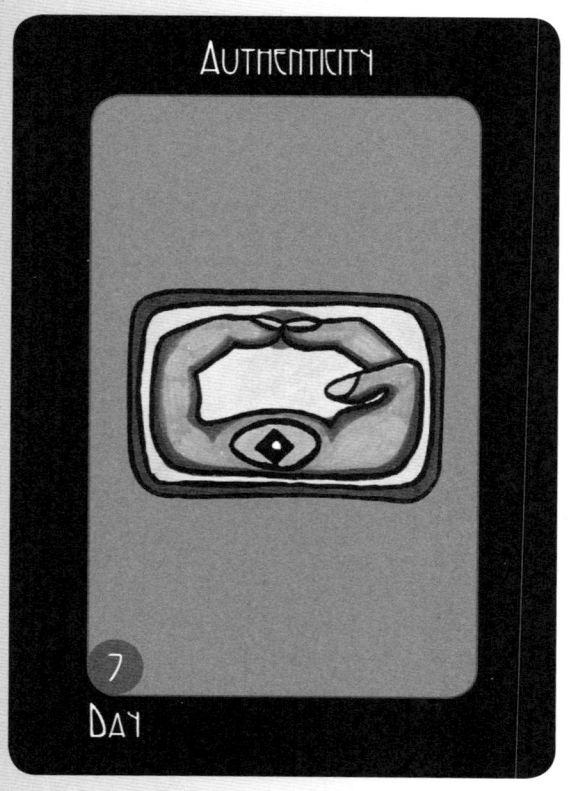

AUTHENTICITY
7 Day

Energy: Spiritual, creative, unconventional.

Day Name: MANIK (mah-Neek).

Direction: West.

Symbol: Deer, timid, sensitive, curious.

Challenge: Learning to be free and secure in your relationships.

Solution: Embrace and find comfort in your individuality, even though it may seem strange to others.

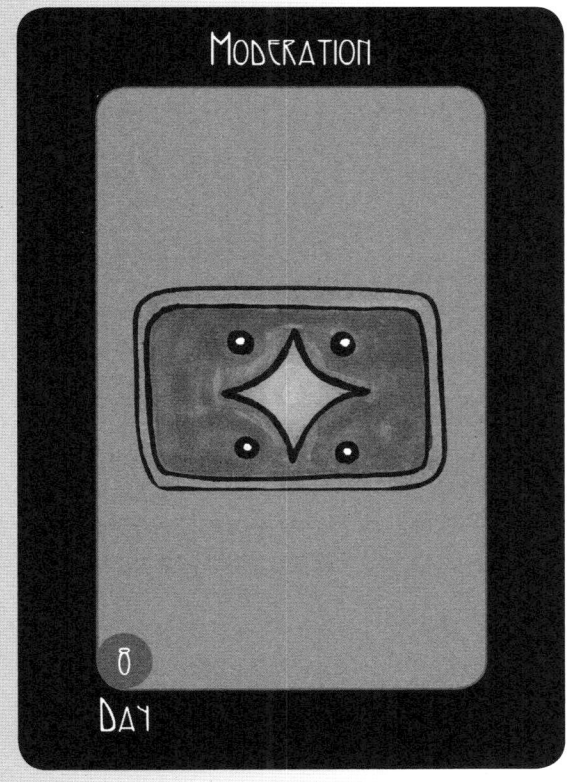

MODERATION
8 Day

Energy: Lucky, productive, green thumb.

Day Name: LAMAT (la-Maht).

Direction: South.

Symbol: Venus, sunset, competition, risk-taking, confrontation.

Challenge: Strive to control excesses and extremes in yourself. Finish what you start.

Solution: Pick your friends and lovers with discernment. Do all things in moderation.

PERSISTENCE
9 Day

Energy: Emotional, imaginative, irrational urges.

Day Name: MULUC (moo-Luke).

Direction: East.

Symbol: Water, jade, change, difficult, challenge between emotions and everyday living.

Challenge: Learning self-control and what triggers "less-than" behavior. Taking personal responsibility for your actions and behavior.

Solution: Develop persistence while being consistent and responsible for your part in all things.

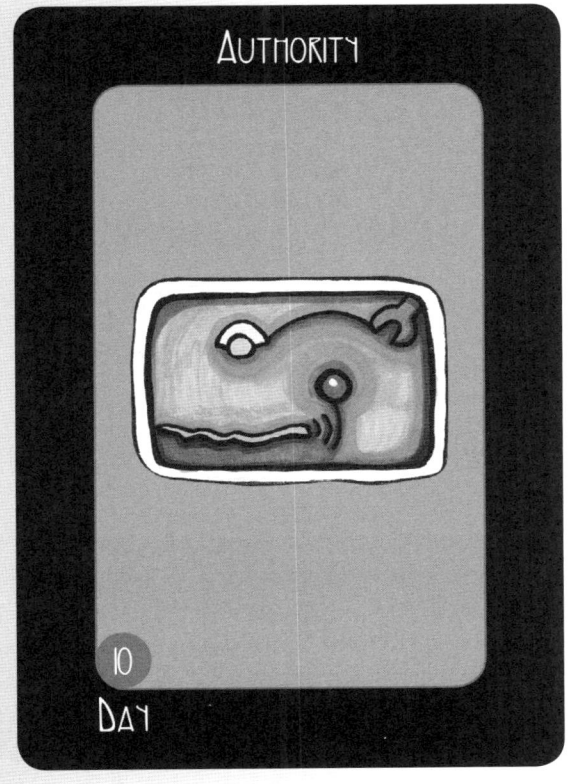

AUTHORITY
10 Day

Energy: Cooperation, enduring, loyal, persistence, stubbornness.

Day Name: OC (oak).

Direction: North.

Symbol: Dog, guides the night sun through the Underworld, celebration.

Challenge: Overcome father/authority issues and attain emotional maturity.

Solution: Develop patience, practice patience, and learn to follow directions from others.

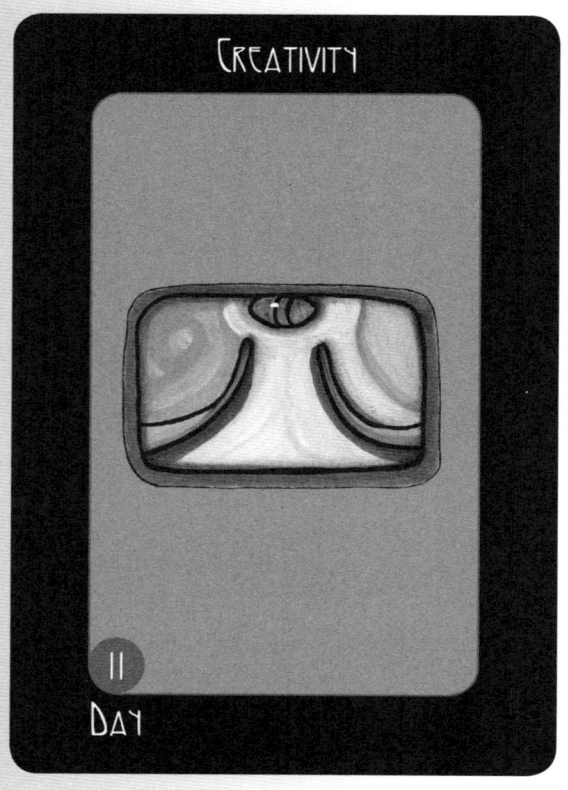

CREATIVITY
II Day

Energy: Artistic, egocentric, having multiple interests.

Day Name: CHUEN (chew-En).

Direction: West.

Symbol: Howling monkey, craftsman, patron of arts, and knowledge.

Challenge: Become proficient with one thing at a time. Avoid being self absorbed while exploring your creative potential.

Solution: Strive to become intimate with nature as a "portal way" to your other creative endeavors.

EMOTIONS
12 Day

Energy: Concern for future generations, low profile.

Day Name: EB (abe).

Direction: South.

Symbol: Grass, associated with rain and storms, healing rifts, and settling differences.

Challenge: Do not suppress anger and learn to resolve it creatively.

Solution: "Know Thyself" and learn to be honest and open about your feelings.

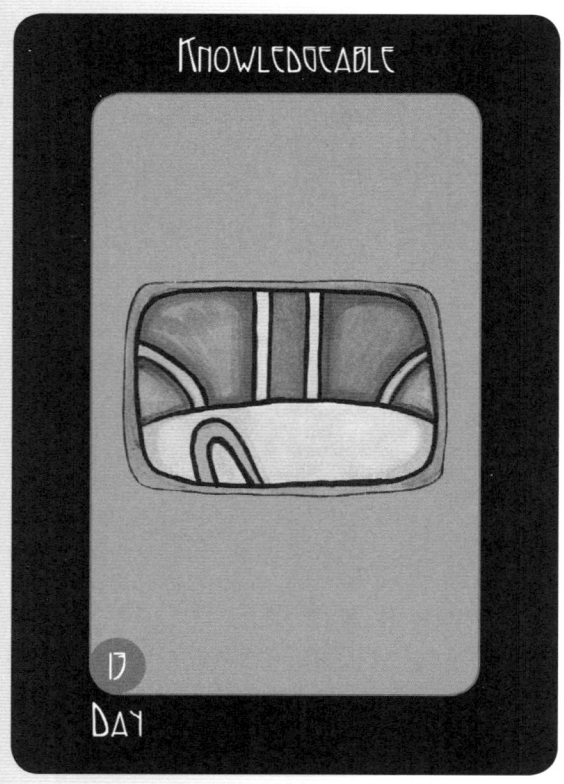

KNOWLEDGEABLE
13 Day

Energy: Authoritative, competent, mediation.

Day Name: BEN (bane).

Direction: East.

Symbol: Reed, fosters growth of corn, cane, and man.

Challenge: Develop discernment and flexibility in all things.

Solution: Learn to compromise and develop social skills.

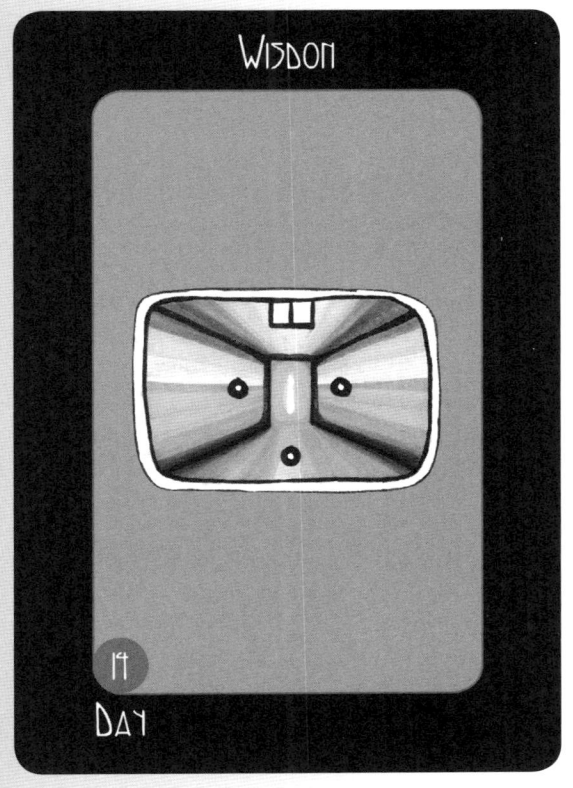

WISDOM
14 Day

Energy: Intelligent, psychic, sensitive, secretive.

Day Name: IX (eesh).

Direction: North.

Symbol: The Night Jaguar-Sun, find insights.

Challenge: Sharing clear and honest communication without personal relationship entanglements.

Solution: Develop healing and counseling skills.

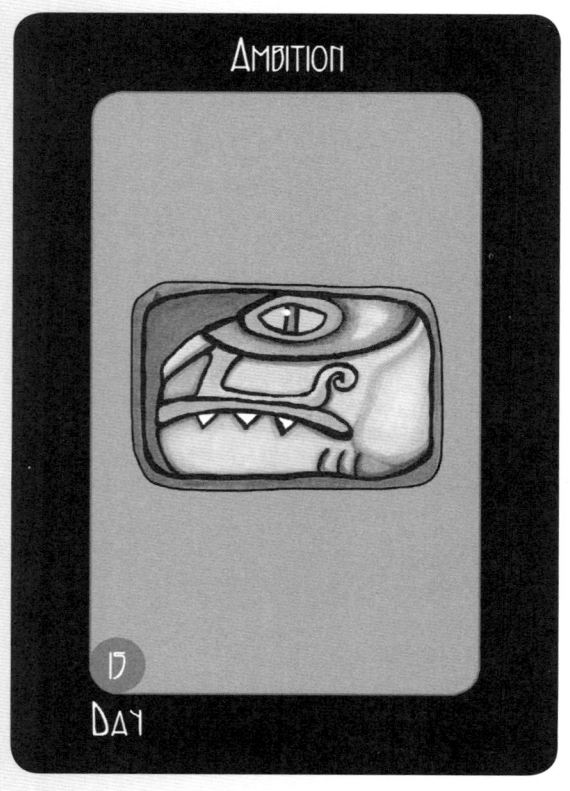

AMBITION
15 Day

Energy: Independent, discriminating, ambitious, escapist.

Day Name: MEN (mane)

Direction: West.

Symbol: Eagle, the wise-one, far-seeing, moon, favors self-interest, thinks a lot, talks detail.

Challenge: Create a life that includes both freedom and companionship.

Solution: Gain a deeper knowledge and understanding of human nature.

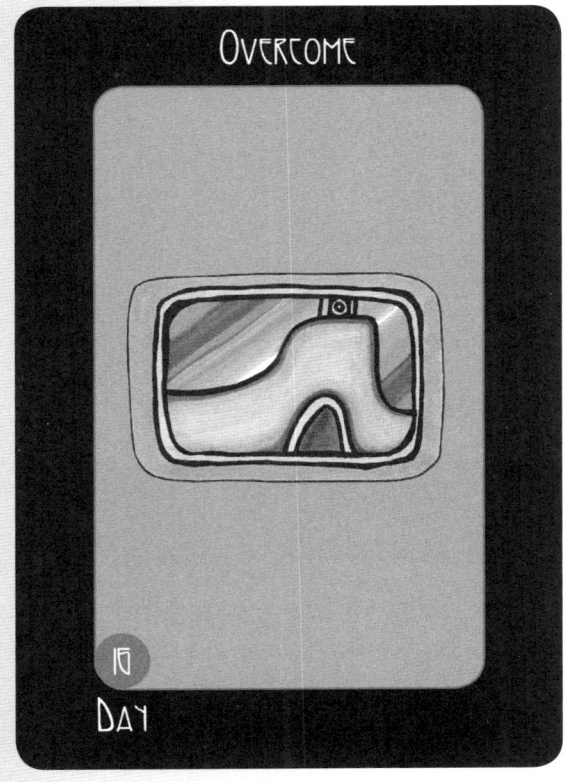

OVERCOME
16 Day

Energy: Serious, deep, wise.

Day Name: CIB (keeb).

Direction: South.

Symbol: Owl/vulture, death-birds of night and day, wax soul, insect, strong-willed, sensitive, what is real and what is not.

Challenge: Overcome self-consciousness, insecurities, and issues of self-worth.

Solution: Get to work, create excellence in chosen field or endeavor.

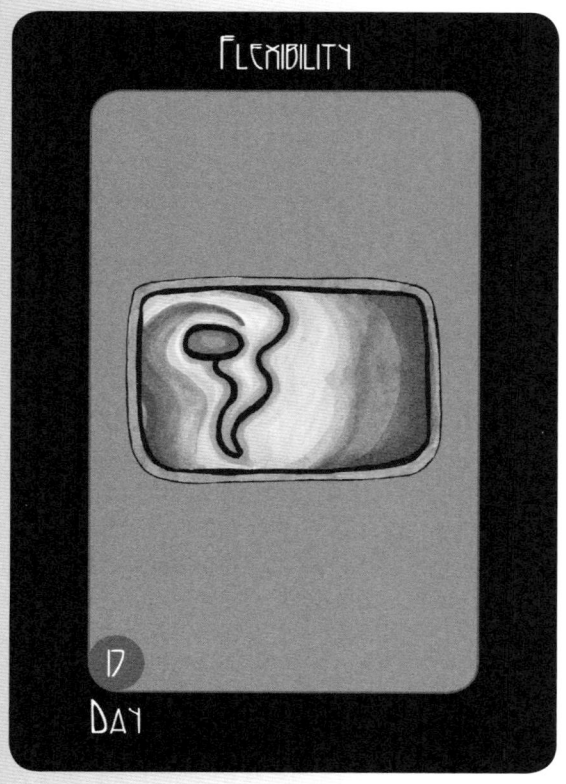

FLEXIBILITY
17 Day

Energy: Mental, pragmatic.

Day Name: CABAN (ka-Bane).

Direction: East.

Symbol: Earthquake, formidable power, season, thought, dreamer, and manifestor.

Challenge: Learn to live within a reasonable plan.

Solution: Strive to be more patient and tolerant.

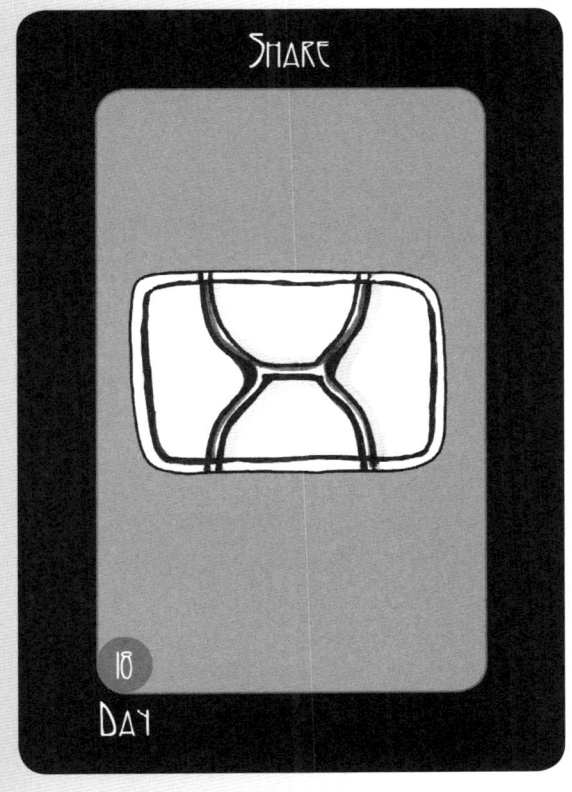

SHARE
18 Day

Energy: Practical, coordinated, "black or white" or "right or wrong."

Day Name: ETZNAB (ets-Nob).

Direction: North.

Symbol: Knife, obsidian sacrificial knife, tough choices or decisions.

Challenge: Tendency to choose self-interest over self-sacrifice.

Solution: Allow others to take leadership role and learn to share.

CURIOSITY
19 Day

Energy: Youthful, friendly, openness to nature and mysteries of the universe.

Day Name: CAUAC (cow-ahk).

Direction: West.

Symbol: Storm, celestial dragon serpents, gods of thunder and lightening, freedom and dependency.

Challenge: Resolve contradictions between freedom and a need to belong, at times, resulting in dependency.

Solution: Develop ability and skills to teach and heal. Find an apprenticeship with a master.

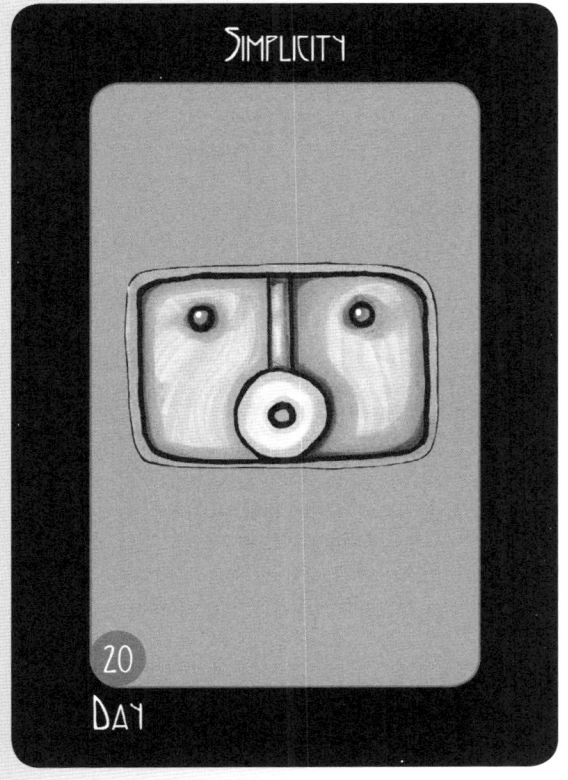

SIMPLICITY
20 Day

Energy: Artistic, dreamy, idealistic, romantic.

Day Name: AHAU (ah-Haw).

Direction: South.

Symbol: Sun, the radiant sun god, religion, and arts.

Challenge: Learn to handle disappointments due to unrealistic expectations. Learn to tolerate unfairness in others.

Solution: Simplicity in all things in heaven and on Earth.

Chapter 5

Surfing the Overworlds

Initiation, 1 Overworld
Duality, 2 Overworld
Action, 3 Overworld
Stability, 4 Overworld
Empowerment, 5 Overworld
Flow, 6 Overworld
Reflection, 7 Overworld

Balance, 8 Overworld
Patience, 9 Overworld
Manifest, 10 Overworld
Clarity, 11 Overworld
Transformation, 12 Overworld
Completion, 13 Overworld

With the concept of Overworlds and the number 13, we would like for you to think "as above, so below." According to Maya elder Gerardo Barrios, the sacred number 13 corresponds to thirteen joints in the human body, (1 neck, 2 shoulders, 2 elbows, 2 wrists, 2 hips, 2 knees, 2 ankles), which serve as points of exchange between the cosmos and humans. The Maya also observed thirteen stages of maturation and transformation that a seed exhibits on its way to becoming mature fruit. It is perhaps viable then to assume the cosmos, like the fruit, goes through the same ripening process, and like the seeds of a fruit, begin and end the cycle over and over again.

It is thought that the joints in the human body are the exchange points where cosmic energy enters and informs the physical body. They also believed that the 20 digits, our fingers and toes were emanating our energy back out into the cosmos and connected us to the Earth and the heavens much like an energetic spider web. And there is no question about the changing or ripening energy of fruit. We can observe the changes brought about by the interaction of sunlight and rain as the fruit grows and ripens.

The thirteen Overworld cards represent the transformation of consciousness. The nine Underworld cards represent the evolution of consciousness. As we encounter transformational energy (Overworld energy), the physical brain changes to accommodate the new awareness (Underworld energy). And as the brain changes, so does the body. From a larger view, we can look at the physical and mental/emotional evolution of humankind and compare it to the energies described by the Maya and see the distinct evolutionary correlations. They were looking at a much larger picture.

When you think of the Overworlds or Underworlds, try not to think in a directional sense but rather orbits within orbits. Consider that the different energies combine to give us an attitude or action in the Middleworld or Earth plane. With the Overworld and Underworld idea, consider that the ancients envisioned that the Underworld would surface at night to devour the light of the sun and the sun would in turn re-emerge to illuminate the darkness once again. These actions are noted on the cards and you can use the night and day marking to help distinguish whether the issue at hand lives in the light of day or is rather operating in the shadow of darkness. If it is a night sign, one might consider working within the subconscious, to heal an imbalance.

Each of the thirteen Overworlds is ruled by a deity with specific qualities. Because we have no record of the Mayan visuals or names for these deities, we have used Aztec images.

The Maya had 15-17 calendars that we know of, which worked together in a synchronized manner to forecast everything from the spiritual quality of any particular day in the distant future to agriculture and warfare, and optimal times for conception of future generations. These are only a few of the earthly concerns the calendars addressed.

Bear in mind, all levels of consciousness described within this deck are intertwined. Our experience of the energies described works in synchronicity for our souls' evolution. The energies described in the 13 Overworlds are 13 levels of understanding. Each of the 13 levels of understanding must be realized to progress through one level of the nine Underworlds which will be described in the next chapter.

As you look at the Major Arcana and the Day cards, those will be more rapidly transiting energies as we consider what the cards tell us about our more current mental attitude or fixed ideas that tend to keep us from evolving or those energies that are supporting our progress.

Remember, as you meander through the images and ideas, that energy/spirit informs and designs all of material reality. These symbols are the energies and attitudes that they believed emanated from the cosmos to affect matters here on Earth.

It is not such a strange idea for those who have utilized astrology as a guide to understanding their lives. For those who don't understand it, consider the ebb and flow of the ocean tides as affected by the moon or planting by the phases of the moon.

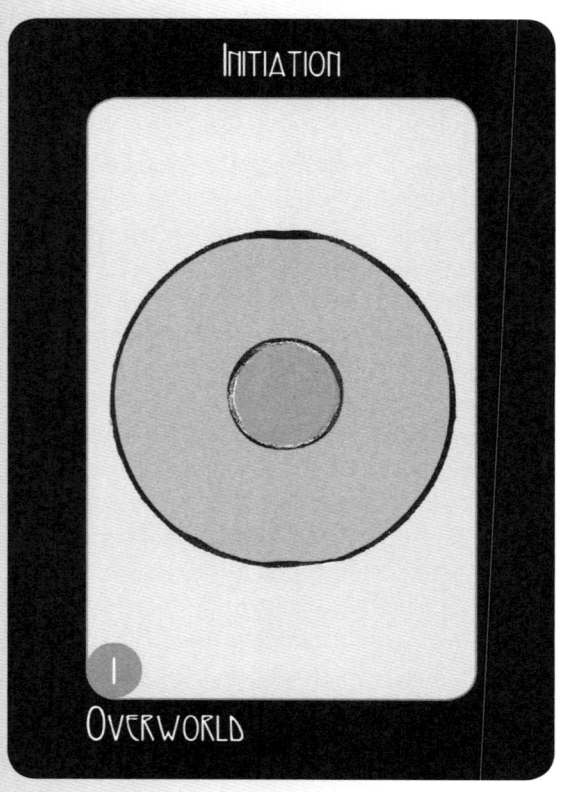

INITIATION
1 Overworld

Key: Beginning, initiation, conception.

Traits: Assertive, Self-guided.

Energy: Artistic, dreamy, idealistic, romantic.

Maya Number: HUN (1).

Ruling God: Xiuhtecuhtli—Aztec god of fire and time.

Positive Aspect: We read the energy of Hun or the first Overworld, as initiatory. This card in a spread could indicate a strong and grand beginning to a project, relationship, or idea. Fire is a volatile and energetic sign, so the energy to accomplish and illuminate any idea is available.

Generally speaking, in a positive position, Hun can be an adventurous, excited spiritual essence that brings light and joy to any new beginning. Think of a seed of maize, within its construct it has all of the information it needs to sprout, flower, and ripen and regenerate itself. The energy of this card is similar; we have in place all that we need to blossom and thrive.

Negative Aspect: We can interpret Hun as a volatile energy that can disturb the peace of an evolving idea, project, or situation. Also in its shadow position, Hun can be an impediment to completion rather than a thrust toward completion. If you are already in a new relationship, business venture, or project, it could necessitate starting again from the beginning and let the inherent flow that is already present guide you. Don't get too mental or try to re-create creation. In short, get out of the way and let native intelligence lead.

History: Xiuhtecuhtli (she wa te KWA tlee) is also known as the "Turquoise Lord" or "Lord of Fire;" he was the god of fire, day, and heat. He was the lord of volcanoes and the personification of life after death. Xiuhtecuhtli represents warmth in cold, light in darkness, and food during famine.[1]

According to the Florentine Codex, Xiuhtecuhtli is a manifestation of Ometecuhtli, the "Lord of Duality" or the mother and father of Gods who dwelled in the turquoise enclosure in the center of Earth. A sacred fire was always kept burning in the temples of Xiuhtecuhtli. In gratitude for the gift of fire, the first mouthful of food from each meal was flung into the hearth.[2]

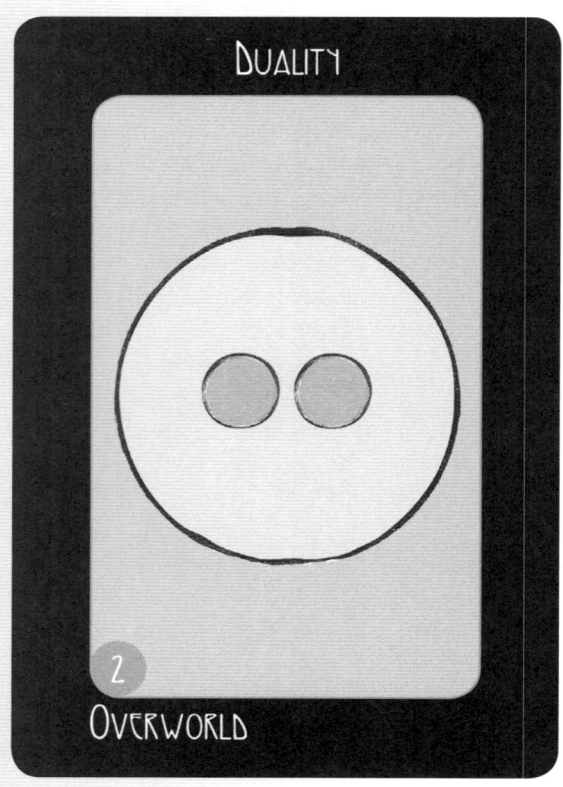

DUALITY
2 Overworld

Key: Centered-self, all one, harmony, walk in balance.

Traits: Sensitive to extremes, recognition when separating self from Creator Spirit.

Energy: Balance between opposing dualities.

Maya Number: KA (2)

Ruling God: Tlaltecuhtli—Aztec god of Earth.

Positive Aspect: Since we emanate from union, it is always our desire to return to that source and state of wholeness. It is a wise being that can distinguish the duality of earthly experience and proceed through life with an understanding that our challenge here is to remember union.

For instance, if you are fighting with your lover, it is not the other that is causing you pain. As part of divine creation, the two of you are inseparable. You both emanate from the Great Spirit. Knowing this then, one must review their own perspective on the issue and how they create the duality or opposition. The energy of this card allows one to recognize that the tools of overcoming separation are at hand. You have the innate understanding to overcome the separation. The energetic forces surrounding you are supporting you.

Negative Aspect: When we feel threatened or fearful of outside forces, we easily become victims of any given situation. In the negative placement of this card, one is encouraged to take responsibility for their thought process and to recognize that they alone can create harmony by understanding they are not outside of the circle of events or circumstances. There are no victims.

History: Tlaltecuhtli (tlal te KWa tlee) is the Aztec god of Earth. The energy embodied is that of catalysis; creating a reaction.[3]

Most Aztec representations depict this creature as female, despite the male gender of the name. Usually in a birthing squat, her obsidian-blade mouth open; according to the *Histoire du Mexique*, she is being escorted from the Overworld to Earth by Quetzalcoatl and Tezcatlipoca who have turned themselves into serpents. One grasps the right hand and left foot and the other takes the left hand and right foot. They squeeze Tlaltecuhtli until her body is debilitated. They take one half away to the sky and the other half they use to form the surface of the Earth. They make her hair trees and grasses; and her skin, flowers. Her eyes become wells and fountains and little caves and her nose and shoulders become valleys and mountains. She cries many times in the night desiring to eat the hearts of men and will not be quiet until she gets fruit sprinkled with the blood of men.[4]

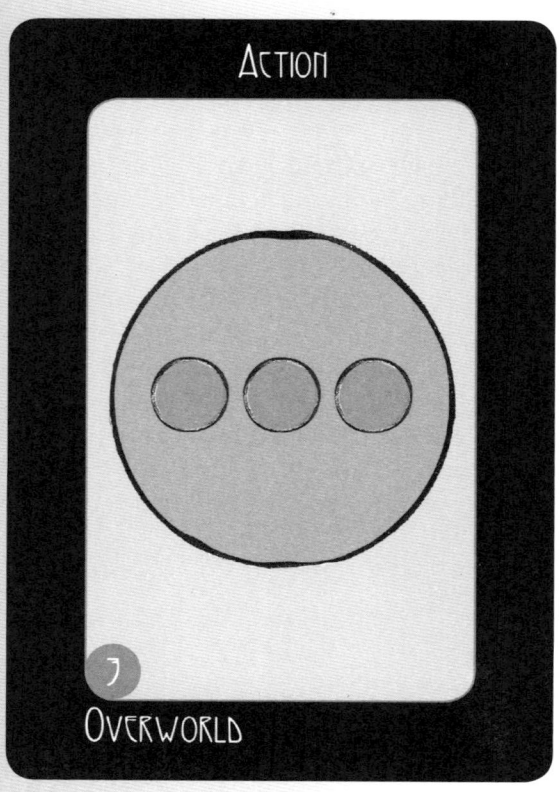

ACTION
3 Overworld

Key: Movement, expression, restless.

Traits: Eloquent self expression embodies motion.

Energy: Action, motion, germination.

Maya Number: OX (3)

Ruling God: Chalchiuhtlicue—Aztec goddess of water and childbirth.

Positive Aspect: When this card is in a reading, the seeker is being reminded of their grace and elegance. It re-calls us to the healing, transforming waters of Chalchiuhtlicue (chahl chee oo TLEE kway) to remember that we are from the ONE and that misery cannot manifest or reign when we remember who we are and where we come from. This card may indicate that your natural propensity for grace in communication is needed. At this moment, clarity and coherence in you communication skills is present.

Negative Aspect: A refusal to recognize that we are endowed with all we need to survive and thrive. Negatively placed, this card can indicate a clumsiness and impatience in all areas of self expression and movement. It is time to slow down, re-group, and bask in the blessings offered from every direction. Until you can access the eloquence of your own truth, back up for a moment, and find your peace before disturbing someone else.

History: Chalchiuhtlicue is the Aztec goddess of water and childbirth. Chalchiuhtlicue, "she of the jade skirt,"[5] is the goddess of lakes, streams, and baptism. One of the images that represents her is "a river from which grew a prickly pear cactus laden with fruit, symbolizing the human heart."[6]

Chalchiuhtlicue was ruling god of the 4th Sun, which she destroyed by "releasing 52 years of rain to flood the Earth. She also protected humanity by changing the people into fish so that the waters would not drown them, and by creating a bridge linking Earth to heaven for those in her favor."[7]

In Central Mexican birth ceremonies[8], Chalchiuhtlicue plays a major role in baptism. Over a period of several days, a midwife would perform ritual baths and offer the goddess prayers for the newborn infant's protection.

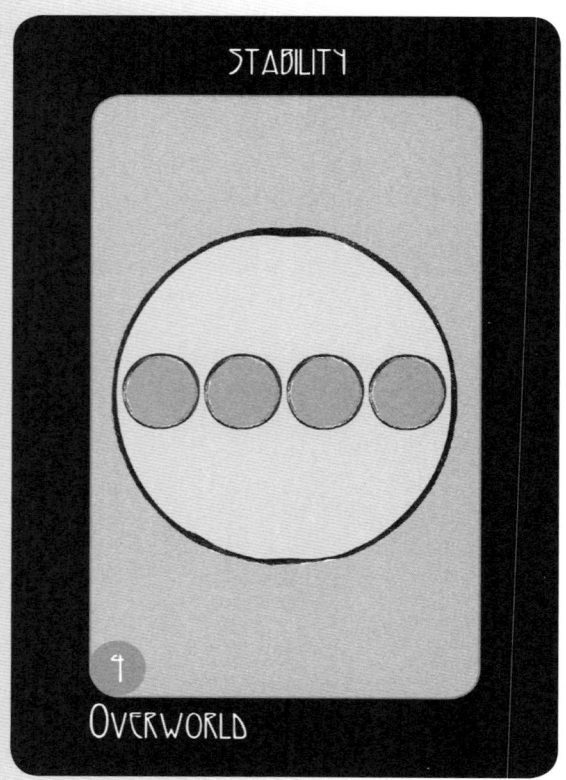

STABILITY
4 Overworld

Key: Four dimensions, grounding, stable.

Traits: Patient, stable, clarity.

Energy: Grounded, stable, firmly anchored.

Maya Number: KAN (4).

Ruling God: Tonatiuh—Aztec god of the sun and warriors.

Positive Aspect: This card in a beneficial position highlights strength and stability brought to any situation. The person or situation is an anchoring force for progress and clarity and demands the best from people in any given situation. One can relax in knowing that the best effort given at this time will generate desired results.

Negative Aspect: In its shadow aspect, this card can signal ruthlessness and point out a highly impatient and critical person. In the quest for understanding this situation, it is best to review exactly what is required of you for you to realize optimal results. Are you being too critical and demanding? Do you need to clarify your expectations and goals? Make a list for yourself and contemplate what is realistic at this time.

History: Tonatiuh (TO na TE wa) was a "fierce and warlike god... He typically appears with red body paint, an eagle feather headdress and a large rayed solar disk."[9] He is the god of the east to the Maya.[10]

To the Aztecs, Tonatiuh was the "leader of Tollan, heaven."[11] Also, he was the god of the fifth sun. "According to their cosmology, each sun was a god with its own cosmic era. According to their creation myth, the god demanded human sacrifice as tribute and without it, would refuse to move through the sky."[12]

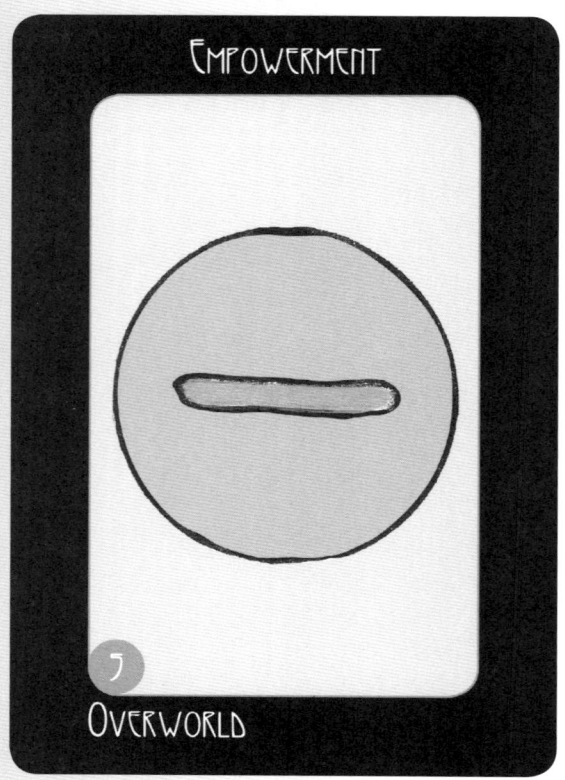

EMPOWERMENT
5 Overworld

Key: Purification, forgiveness, sexuality.

Traits: Self-forgiveness, insightful, compassionate.

Energy: Compassionate, purifying, sexual, empowering.

Maya Number: HO (5)

Ruling God: Tlazolteotl—Aztec goddess of purification, steam bath, midwives and filth (sin).

Positive Aspect: In a well-dignified position, this card can indicate keen and clear insight. This can indicate a wise and forgiving person and one who has developed compassion and understanding by living and learning. Their clarity and understanding have a healing quality which leads others into self forgiveness, understanding, and acceptance.

Negative Aspect: The shadow side of this card is a blind, reckless greed that perpetuates individual desire and need.

The propensity for self-inflicted violence and betrayal in this position should be a warning sign to do things differently to avoid loss and destruction.

History: Tlazolteotl (tla sol TE otl) is the Aztec goddess of purification, steam bath, midwives, filth, and a patroness of adulterers.[13] "In Nahuatl, the word tlazolli can refer to vice and diseases."[14]

Tlazolteotl was the goddess of filth (sin), vice, and sexual misdeeds. She was thought to cause sexually transmitted diseases if "forbidden love" was indulged and those involved were considered unclean "on both a physical and moral level."[15]

"However, she was a purification goddess as well, who forgave the sins and disease of those caused by misdeeds, particularly sexual misdeeds. Her dual nature is seen in her epithets; Tlaelquani ('she who eats filth and sin'), and Tlazomiquiztli, ('the death caused by lust'), and Ixcuinan, ('she who has two faces')."[16] Cures could be found through rites of purification, steam-baths, and "calling upon Tlazolteotl (the goddess of love and desire)."[17]

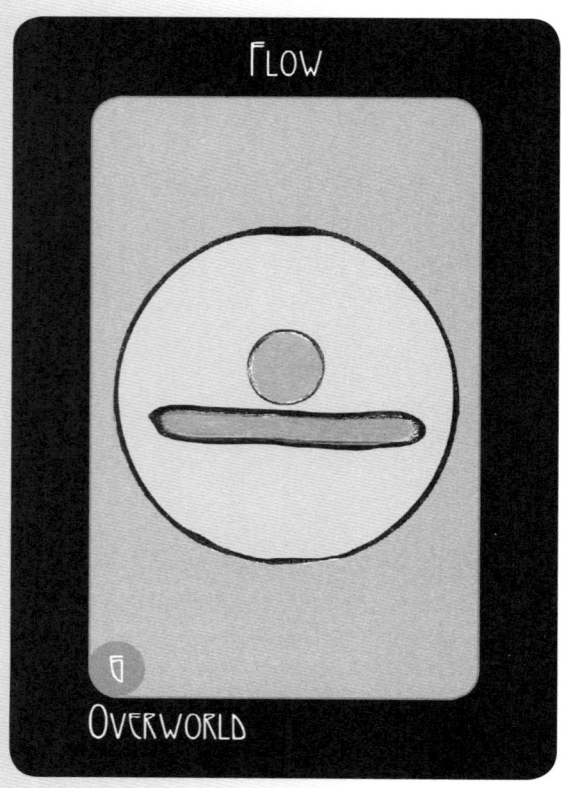

FLOW
6 Overworld

Key: Enlightenment, peace, flow.

Traits: Facilitator, athletic or physically active, self-awareness.

Energy: Fluidity, negotiation, responsiveness.

Maya Number: UAC (6)

Ruling God: Mictlantecuhtli—the Mesoamerican god of Death.

Positive Aspect: It is through activity and motion that this idea can lend consolidating energies to any situation. If something is on the brink of dying and laboring to do so, this card can indicate a beneficial cathartic energy to push the issue through the energetic bottleneck towards resurrection. Life is movement, evolution. However, chaotic movement is not the goal. We want a smooth and graceful transition from ignorance to enlightenment.

Negative Aspect: Through non-awareness, this card can indicate a destructive clumsiness and recklessness. When expressed in this manner, one is urged to pull back from any issue inquired about and reassess what their ultimate goal is. Find your peace amid the chaos and proceed with caution.

History: Mictlantecuhtli (meek tlahn tay COO tlee) the Aztec god of death, usually appears as a "skeleton of bleached white bones with red bloody spots. He is often festooned with owl feathers, paper head ornaments and banners, and wears a collar of extruded eyeballs."[18] Though such imagery might seem morbid today, in the Aztec world skeletal imagery was a symbol of fertility, health, and abundance.[19] This created close symbolic links between death and life.

Death gods were considered fundamentally stupid and often fell for the tricks of smarter gods. In the creation story of the twin gods, Quetzalcoatl and Xolotl, they journey to Mictlan, Mictlantecuhtli first promises to return the bones of previous mankind, and then runs away with the bones. Quetzalcoatl chases Mictlantecuhtli, retrieves the bones but unfortunately drops them, "thus yielding a race of humans of mixed sizes."[20] Mictlantecuhtli ruled over Mictlan, "place of the dead"[21] and "the lowest and northernmost section of the underworld."[22]

"In the Aztec codices Mictlantecuhtli is often depicted with his skeletal jaw open to receive the stars that descend into him during the daytime."[23] Mictlantecuhtli and Mictecacihuatl were the opposites and compliments of Ometecuhtli and Omecihuatl, the givers of life.[24]

REFLECTION
7 Overworld

Key: Integrity, truth, revelation.

Traits: Sense of ethics and integrity, be a "mirror of truth."

Energy: Revelation, proliferation, fearlessness.

Maya Number: UUC (7)

Ruling God: Cinteotl—Aztec god of maize and sustenance.

Positive Aspect: In a positive position, this card can indicate one's unrestrained ability to produce and multiply resources. There is a sense of abundance and gratitude that pervades all things and a sense of well being that cannot be diminished. This is truly where we need to be during times of challenge, since the energy of lacking anything can cause self doubt and fear. It is this celebratory attitude that generates more sustenance, on every level, for us, and our people. In a word, the concept is gratitude.

Negative Aspect: The fear of not having enough can be the indication when this card is poorly placed. Fear begets fear and losses increase when that is where we focus our consciousness. This aspect should encourage the seeker to reassess what is right in their life, what is working, and how life has supported and sustained them.

History: Cinteotl (then tE O'tl) is the Aztec god of maize and sustenance.[25] Cinteotl was brought to this world by Quetzalcoatl and is associated with the group of stars known commonly today as the Pleiades.[26]

Festivals included processions of Aztec women who would dance in the maize fields, bare-breasted, hair down with gratitude for Cinteotl's work. "Usually, at least five newly ripened maize cobs were picked by the older Aztec woman. These were then carried on the female's backs after being carefully wrapped up, somewhat like a mother would wrap up a newborn child. Once the cobs reached their destination, usually outside a house, they were placed in a special corn basket and would stay there until the following year. This was meant to represent the resting of the maize spirits until the next harvesting period came around."[27]

Maize was a staple food throughout the history of Mesoamerican civilization. Many historical sources site the cultivation of corn to be used in sacrifices to the Gods. Sacrifices to the gods were used to ensure the continued "flow of divine power needed to keep the natural world functioning: the sun rising, the rain clouds forming and unloading their cargo, the land giving birth to maize plants."[28]

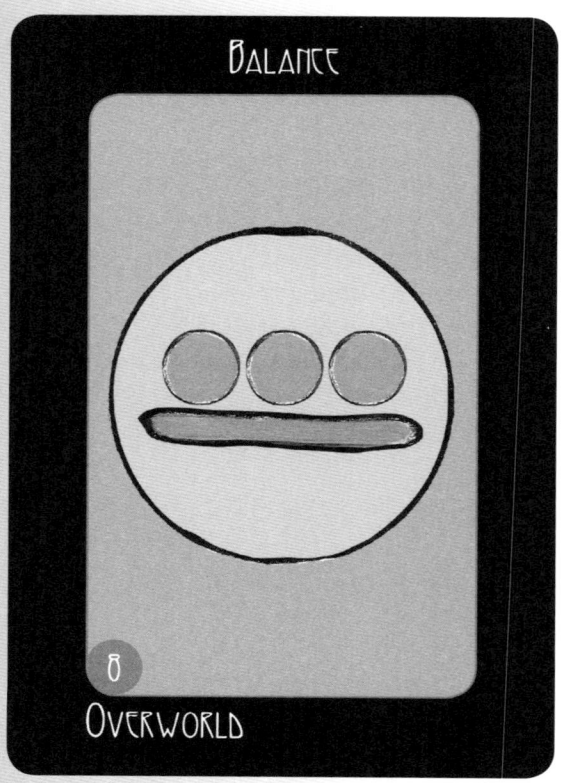

BALANCE
8 Overworld

Key: Harmony, protection.

Traits: Fairness, balance of justice, clear vision, protective.

Energy: Harmony.

Maya Number: UAXAC (8)

Ruling God: Tlaloc Aztec god of the war and rain/ lightning.

Positive Aspect: When this card pertains to a person, one can be comforted about being safe and protected. With the energies governed by the eagle, there is clear vision; the ability to rise above petty obstacles and a fierce commitment to what is right and just. If this card describes business or earthly endeavors, there will be levity and integrity as guiding forces.

Negative Aspect: When this card appears in a negative position or is dignified by surrounding cards that are challenging, it indicates an air of criticism that can be injurious. The criticism is the distortion of the natural tendency towards balance and fairness. In a negative position this card can indicate a scam or deception. If this card falls in a position that describes your actions, re-evaluate your motivations for any action surrounding the issue at hand.

History: Tlaloc (tla LoK) is the Aztec god of the rain and war.[29] The Aztecs portray Tlaloc with serpentine lightning bolts in contrast to the Maya Chac depiction which is clearly part jaguar.[30] "In Post-classic Mexico, Tlaloc was believed to reside in mountain caves. These caves were considered to be miraculous treasure houses filled with wealth and prosperity. To the Aztecs, Tlaloc was known as "the provider," and depending on the rains, could be either generous or miserly."[31]

Tlaloc was the ruling god of the third sun, which was destroyed by Quetzalcoatl sending a "rain of fire"[32] to the Earth. Tlaloc was often depicted with goggle eyes and fangs and was "known for having demanded child sacrifices."[33] In the Aztec religion, Tlaloc was a beneficent god who gave life and sustenance but was also feared for his power to send hail, thunder, and lightning; and for being the lord of the powerful element of water.[34]

In Aztec cosmology, the four corners of the universe are marked by "the four Tlalocs," which "both hold up the sky and function as the frame for the passing of time."[35]

In Aztec mythic cosmography, Tlaloc ruled the fourth level (Upper World) or heaven, called Tlalocan (place of Tlaloc).[36] Tlalocan was a paradise and the afterlife destination of those people who died violently from water, lightning, drowning, or waterborne diseases such as leprosy, dropsy, scabies, and gout.[37]

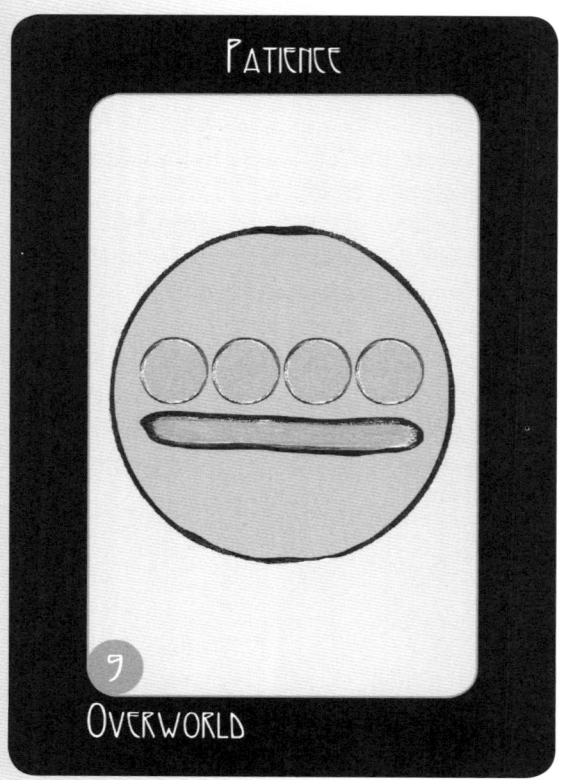

PATIENCE
9 Overworld

Key: Perseverance, completion, patience.

Traits: Ability to see the "big picture," letting go, and completion.

Energy: Budding, forward movement, new life.

Maya Number: BOLON (9)

Ruling God: Quetzalcoatl—Aztec god of light.

Positive Aspect: The appearance of this card indicates a thrust toward a successful completion to a recent effort. It can be an indicator card that the endeavor, relationship or issue in question is a righteous consideration. Consider it a green light for intensified focus and progress.

Negative Aspect: This card in a negative position could indicate a great impatience on the part of the seeker and a warning to step back and take a long hard look at the endeavor.

History: Quetzalcoatl (kayt sahl KO'tl) is the Aztec god of light.[38] In Mayan languages, the words for snake and sky are identical.[39] Quetzalcoatl, the Zuni Kolowisi, and the Hopi Palulukong are all plumed water serpents that can be identified as bringers of abundance and fertility.[40]

Quetzalcoatl also takes the form of the god of wind, Ehecatl-Quetzalcoatl, the road sweeper of the Tlaloque rain gods—"the wind that brings the rain clouds."[41]

Mesoamerican historian David Carrasco has suggested that the preeminent function of the feathered serpent deity throughout Mesoamerican history was as the patron deity of the urban center, "creator god, the morning star, the wind god, the culture hero, the emblem of priesthood," a god of culture and civilization.[42]

As the Tolpiltzin Quetzalcoatl of Tollan, he was known for refusing to sacrifice human beings, and instead, his offerings were always snakes, birds, and butterflies.[43]

Along with other gods, such a Tezcatlipoca and Tlaloc, Quetzalcoatl was called "Ipalnemohuani," a title reserved for the gods directly involved in the creation, which means "by whom we live." He was known as the inventor of books and the calendar, the giver of maize to mankind, and sometimes as a symbol of death and resurrection."[44]

As creator god, Quetzalcoatl journeyed to Mictlan, the Underworld, and created fifth-world mankind from the bones of the previous races. Like the phoenix rising, he suffers humiliation and destruction, only to resurrect and journey to the Underworlds to retrieve the broken bones of the ancestors. With the help of the Chihuacoatl, the broken bones are ground into flour, moistened with Quetzalcoatl's blood, and shaped into human form.[45]

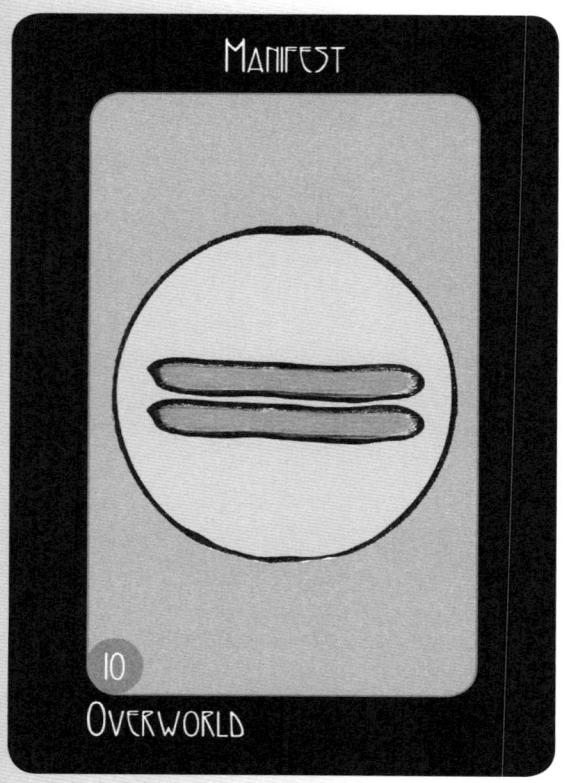

MANIFEST
10 Overworld

Key: Challenge, transformation, manifestation.

Traits: Ability to manifest in the material world with personal responsibility.

Energy: Change through conflict.

Maya Number: LAHUN (10)

Ruling God: Tezcatlipoca—Lord of the Smoking Mirror.

Positive Aspect: In any position, this card, this is a card of challenge and can only be interpreted in a positive light. We don't expand or grow in comfort. We become more authentically who we are designed to be through meeting the challenges before us. If this card comes up in your reading, embrace the challenge and know with the force of Tezcatlipoca, you are being ushered in your optimal capacity and energy as a human being to bring forth your particular gifts for the sake of the planet.

Negative Aspect: Only if you ignore the challenge and retreat from what is beckoning your evolution, can you consider this card a negative influence. In any position, it calls you from reclining position to rise to whatever blocks your progress. This energy requires one to transform challenge into opportunity.

History: Tezcatlipoca (tes kah tlee POH kah) as the Black Tezcatlipoca was brother to Quetzalcoatl, the White Tezcatlipoca.[46] The rivalry between Quetzalcoatl and Tezcatlipoca both collaborated in the manifestation of the different creations. Both of them were seen as instrumental in the creation of life.[47]

Karl Taube and Mary Miller, specialists in Mesoamerican religion, write that: "More than anything, Tezcatlipoca appears to be the embodiment of change through conflict."

Tezcatlipoca is "associated with a wide range of concepts including the night sky, the night winds, hurricanes, the north, the Earth obsidian, enmity, discord, rulership, divination, temptation, jaguars, sorcery, beauty, war, and strife."[48] The "Lord of the Smoking Mirror," Tezcatlipoca, was known for wearing an obsidian mirror in the back of his head, so that he could see what was happening behind him.[49]

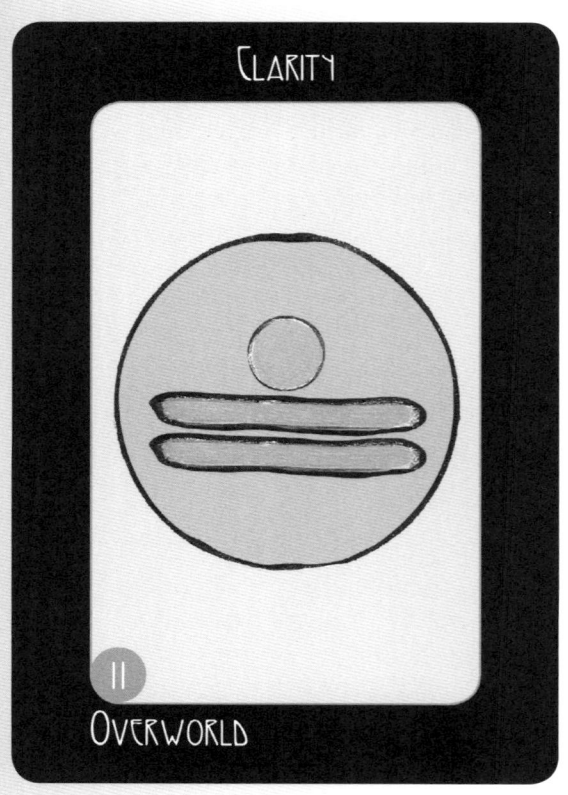

CLARITY
11 Overworld

Key: Clarity, resolution, evolution.

Traits: Capacity for change, simplification, and improvement.

Energy: Flowering.

Maya Number: BULUK (11)

Ruling God: Yohualticitl—Aztec goddess of the moon.

Positive Aspect: In a beneficial placement, this card signifies that the person or present situation is but a reflection of reality, much like the moon reflects the softer quality of the sun's glaring light. It is the ability to decipher through the shadows of reflected light. The awareness and fruition longing to be realized can come with ease.

Negative Aspect: In a poor placement, the seeker is dealing with getting stuck in the darkness, (confusion), therefore not "seeing" the soul's lesson for evolution. Failure to work through this blockage can result in anxiety and feeling alienated from a supportive community.

History: Yohualticitl (yoh-wahl-tee-see-tl) is the Aztec goddess of childbirth.[50] "In Aztec mythology, Metztli (also Meztli, Metzi) was a goddess of the moon, the night, and farmers."[51] This was possibly the same deity as Yohualticitl, Coyolxauhqui, and the male moon god Tecciztecatl.

"The god of worms, who failed to sacrifice himself to become the sun and became the moon instead, his face darkened by a rabbit."[52]

"Metztli, or Yohualticitl (The Lady of Night), was the Mexican goddess of the moon. She had two phases, one is that of a beneficent protectress of harvests and promoter of growth in general, and the other is a bringer of dampness, cold, and ghosts, 'mysterious shapes of the dim half-light of night and its oppressive silence.'"[53]

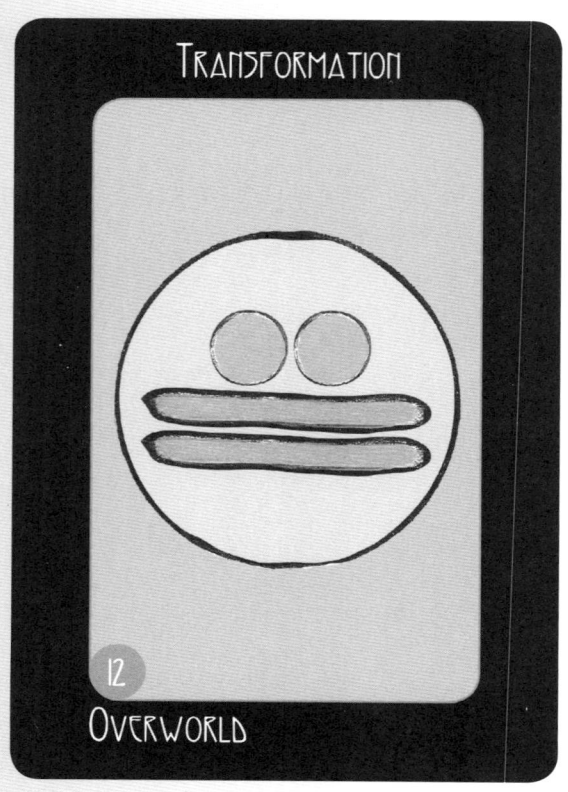

TRANSFORMATION
12 Overworld

Key: New paradigms, retrospection, wisdom.

Traits: Retrospection, transforms parts to new whole.

Energy: Transformation, wisdom.

Maya Number: LAKA (12)

Ruling God: Tlahuizcalpantecuhtli—Mesoamerican god of the morning star.

Positive Aspect: Well dignified, this card can indicate a piercing ability to get to the heart of any matter. It is an indication that the answer to your concerns may come a sa flash of insight or a moment of crystal-clear clarity without your having to obsess or sort through confusing information.

You already have the answer within you. Be still and quiet, re-form the question and listen inwardly; you know exactly what to do.

Negative Aspect: In a negative position, this card can inform you that there is unpredictable chaos brewing because you are not willing to trust your inner knowing. Not to heed the "small, quiet voice inside" could cause untold problems. Listen!

History: Tlahuizcalpantecuhtli (tlah-weets-cahlpahn-tay-coo-tlee) is the Mesoamerican god of the morning star, also known as the Lord of Dawn.[54]

"According to Mesoamerican belief, the rays of the morning star at heliacal rising could inflict great damage upon particular classes of people as well as on maize and water."[55] In some of the codified information (Borgia, Cospi, and Vaticanus B), Venus tables predict the days and victims of the heliacal appearance of the morning star.

In the Leyenda de los Soles, Tlahuizcalpantecuhtli hurls a dart at the newly created sun at Teotihuacán. The new sun god transforms Tlahuizcalpantecuhtli into Itztlacoliuhqui-Ixquimilli, the god of coldness, stone, and castigation.[56]

The Colonial Anales de Cuauhtitlan writes that Quetzalcoatl was burned upon a funeral pyre and reborn as Tlahuizcalpantecuhtli.[57]

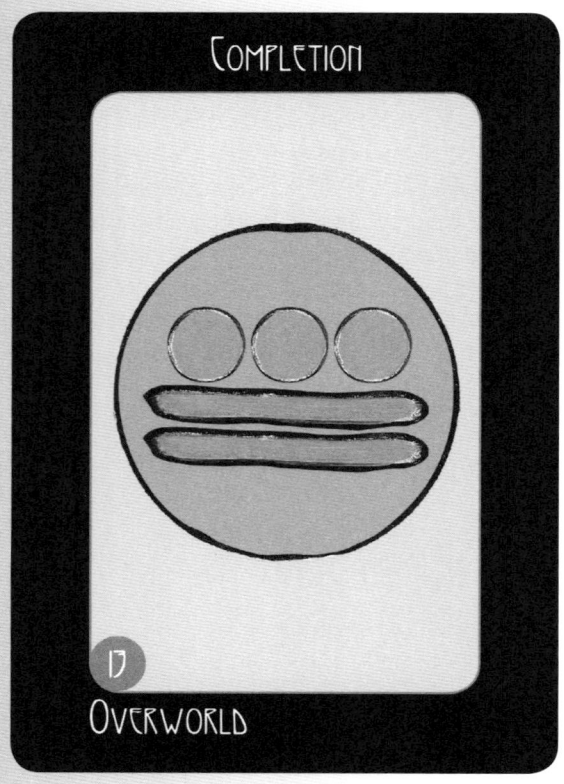

COMPLETION
13 Overworld

Key: Non-dualism, transcendence, completion.

Traits: Commitment, aware of universal support.

Energy: Ascension, expansion, completion.

Maya Number: OXLAHUN (13)

Ruling God: Ometeotl—Aztec supreme god of Creation.

Positive Aspect: When this card comes up in a reading, it could be a good omen for any project or intention you are currently focusing on. It would indicate that the forces of unrelenting tenacity and expansion are with you. It is a signal to commit to the completion of a project or idea so that a higher level of activity may begin. This card would indicate that the question it pertains to is a necessary step in your personal evolution.

Negative Aspect: If Overworld 13 comes up in a poorly placed position, it is time to step back and reconsider your objective. It would indicate that one has lost focus and can progress no further until the confusion and chaos in their thinking is resolved. When it appears in relationship issues, it could indicate that communication is not clear and that the need to "change channels" is necessary. It does not mean that you should stop communicating. At this time, find another subject until you are clear enough to discuss the current issues.

History: Ometeotl (O me TEO tl) is the Aztec supreme deity of creation.[58] The "two-god" Ometeotl embodies the Mesoamerican principle of duality.[59] "This dual, bisexual god rules over the highest heaven of the Nahuatl scheme, Omeyocan, the place of duality."[60] Ometeotl is in the form of Ometecuhtli and his consort Omecihuatl. Together, they are "ever-present progenitors."[61] They send the souls of those about to be born to the surface of the Earth.

"There are no temples dedicated to this god, but references to Ometeotl appear in a number of post-conquest Aztec codices and poetry."[62]

"From the void that was the rest of the universe, the first god, Ometeotl, created itself. Ometeotl was male and female, good and evil, light and darkness, fire and water, judgment and forgiveness, the god of duality.

Ometeotl gave birth to four children, the four Tezcatlipoca's, who each rule over one of the four cardinal directions.

Over the East presides the White Tezcatlipoca, Quetzalcoatl, the god of light, mercy, and wind.

Over the South presides the Blue Tezcatlipoca, Huitzilopochtli, the god of war.

Over the West presides the Red Tezcatlipoca, Xipe Totec, the god of gold, farming, and Spring time.

Over the North presides the Black Tezcatlipoca, Tezcatlipoca, and the god of judgment, night, deceit, sorcery, and the Earth.[63]

Chapter 6

Navigating the Underworlds

Cellular, 1 Underworld
Mammalian, 2 Underworld
Familial, 3 Underworld
Tribal, 4 Underworld
Regional, 5 Underworld

National, 6 Underworld
Global, 7 Underworld
Galactic, 8 Underworld
Universal, 9 Underworld

The most important Mayan pyramids, the Temple of Inscription in Palenque, the Pyramid of the Jaguar in Tikal, and the Pyramid of Kukulcan in Chichén Itza are all representations of the nine levels of consciousness, or the hierarchical structure of the Nine Underworlds. According to Carl Johan Calleman, the Underworlds are related to the sequentially activated crystalline structures in the Earth's inner core. The concept of the Underworlds is representative of the evolution of the human brain. While each new level of awareness completes, one level of consciousness does not replace the other. We achieve the new awareness of all activated levels simultaneously. The significance of the "10-28-2011"[1] date was the completion of the nine underworlds of human evolution.

In each Underworld there are seven days and six nights that are energetic "wave movements"[2] through each level of the Underworld. New creation occurs during the day cycle, while integration happens during the night cycle. We will not be examining these concepts here, but hope to encourage you to look further into the precision with which the Star Gazers forecast the evolution of the physical and spiritual universe. For more in-depth study, you might want to look at Barbara Hand Clow's book, *The Mayan Code*. Each of the nine cycles of the Underworlds is generated by a cycle twenty times shorter than the previous cycle. To give you a consideration of the width and breadth of the Mayan view of time, they have names for evolutionary periods over a 16.4 billion-year span of time. In comparison, the first Underworld of 16.4 billion years of evolution, compared to the Ninth Underworld with 260 days of evolution, is indeed an indescribably rapid transition of consciousness. Do we wonder why we feel that time is evaporating?

The first level of the Nine Underworlds is according to the Maya 16.4 billion years. It was during this period that this planet developed from the "Big Bang" to cellular consciousness. If we compare that to the 7th Underworld, or what is called the planetary consciousness, that period of time is a 256-year period of time. Each level is built on another with a twenty-times shorter duration period than the previous one.

We do ourselves a disservice by looking at the Maya calendar as a portent for the cataclysmic end. It rather suggests that our evolutionary process is speeding up and that the physical universe that defined us, is becoming an old idea as we emerge from matter to light.

If we consider the transition from the Planetary Underworld to the Galactic Underworld, those old paradigms of manipulating the physical world to survive are being replaced with an understanding that consciousness indeed does inform matter. And that what we think and how we perceive reality is the new currency for survival.

For our purposes, each of the Underworld cards can reflect to the reader where their consciousness lies. Are you dealing with an amoebic mentality in relationship or are you so expansive that you avoid getting caught up in a web of personalities? Will you struggle for survival or will you learn to manifest at will, accepting that you are creative energy and cannot be separate from Source?

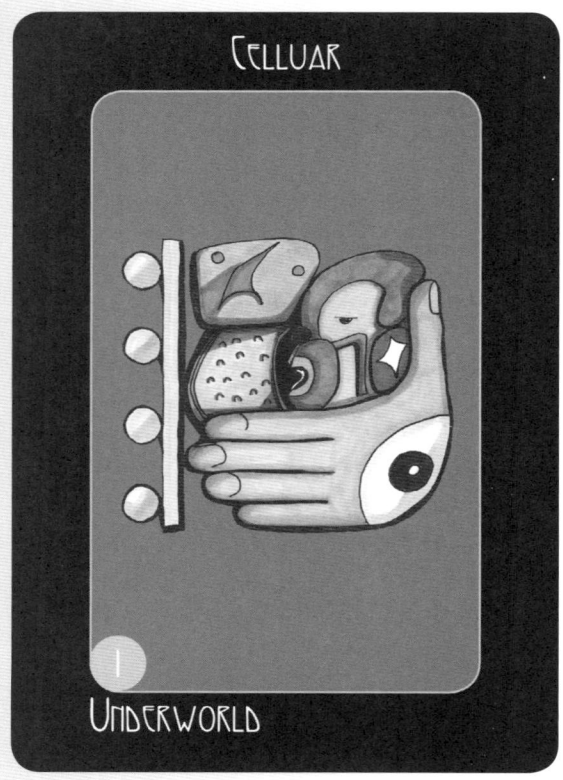

CELLULAR
I Underworld

Key: Birth, body identity.

Energy: Chemical, physical/material world.

Time Period: 16.4 billion years.

Definition: This first phase of evolution is a period of time spanning 16.4 billion years. This unfolding of cellular consciousness not only describes the chemical and cellular evolution, but also the birthing of galaxies, stars, and planets in our solar system. It is of interest that current scientific theory has the "Big Bang" theory occurring 15 billion years ago.

For our purposes, this card represents a preoccupation with physical/material issues with little consciousness of our ability to transform energy. If you have pulled this card in a reading, it is a reminder that you are more than your cellular structure. It is a reflection of naiveté, regarding your place in the cosmos and the power that you carry.

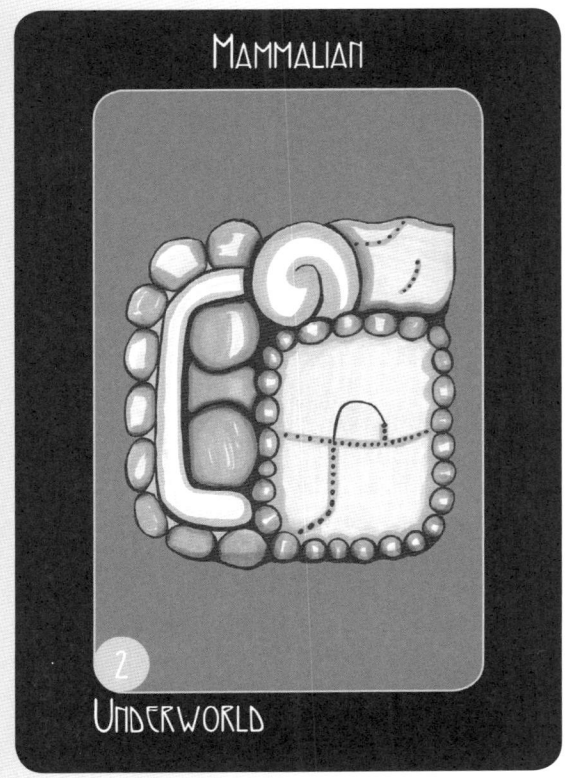

MAMMALIAN
2 Underworld

Key: Primal identity, survival, sexuality.

Energy: Primal instinct.

Time Period: 820 million years.

Definition: The Mammalian Underworld card represents the evolution of multi-cellular organisms, sexual polarity, and the developmental phase of the plant kingdom. This period is an 820-million-year span of time.

If this card comes up in your reading, it would appear that you are functioning from a primal instinct for survival rather than allowing your higher cognitive functions to lead you. It is a time to renegotiate your fears and examine feelings of defensiveness.

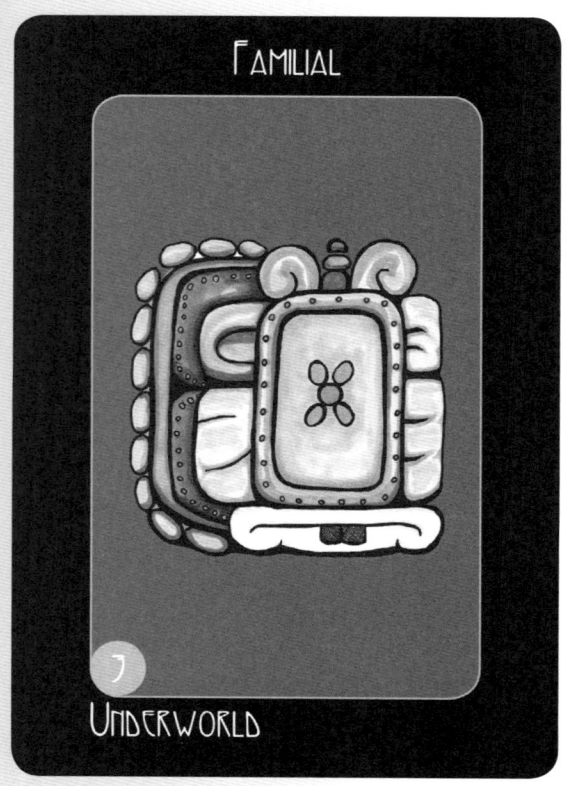

FAMILIAL
3 Underworld

Key: Walking upright, use of tools, boundaries, family identity.

Energy: Family organization, intelligent use of tools.

Time Period: 41 million years.

Definition: The Familial Underworld card refers to a period of time of 41 million years. This is a period of anthropoid consciousness evolution and refers to the organization of family, walking in an upright position, and the intelligent use of tools.

If you are looking at this card in a reading, it is reminding you that you are more than your boundaries suggest. It is one thing to reside within a familial structure, but it is by no means your definition. Look beyond the boundaries, knowing that all of the information you possess from your early relationships and genetics are more than enough equipment to become a citizen of the world, a cosmonaut of the universe.

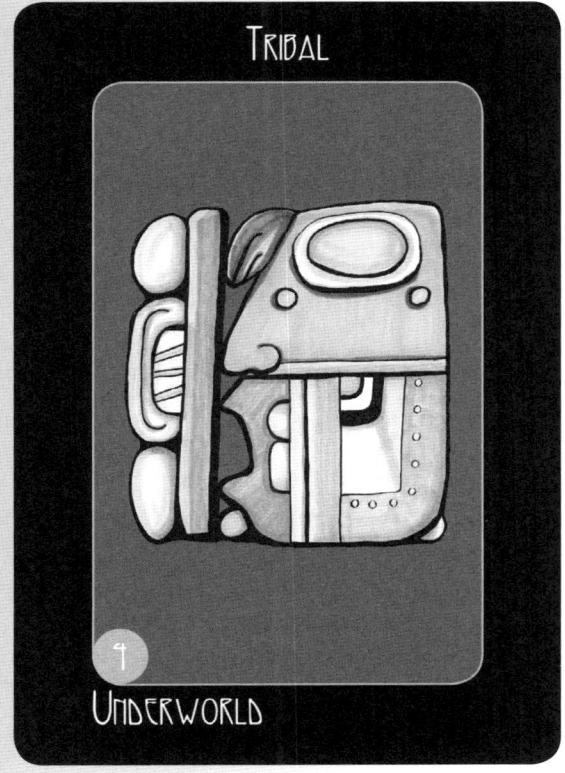

TRIBAL
4 Underworld

Key: Oral language, complex tools, tribal identity.

Energy: Tribal organization, problem solving, rudimentary language.

Time Period: 2 million years.

Definition: The beginning of this 2-million-year period was the dawning of Homo sapiens who were capable of creating complex tools and bringing forth a simple, oral language. Throughout this time, tribal organization was, and is, a construct for our evolving species.

   This card would indicate that you are not yet comfortable with a broader definition. You may have physical tools and know how to use them, but the message is to recognize that there are many more, non-physical tools that can be employed. This card is calling you to higher-level thinking about the problems that challenge you. Don't be limited by definitions.

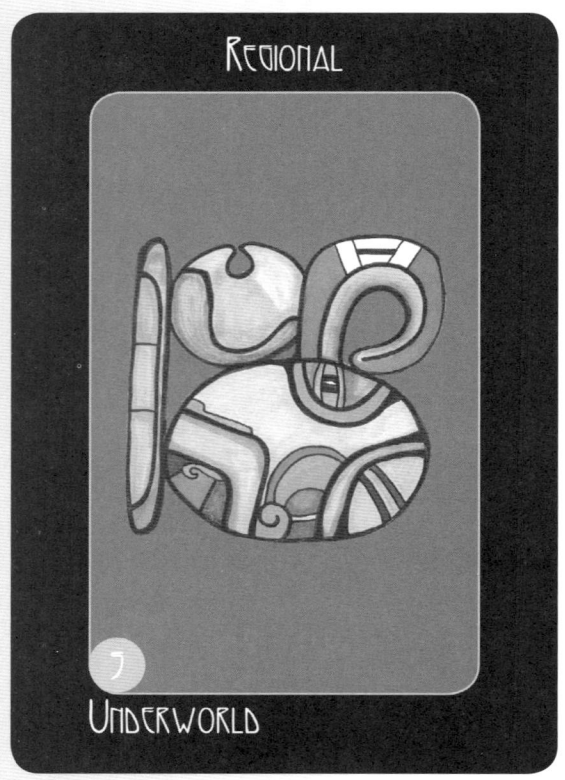

REGIONAL
5 Underworld

Key: Complex language, culture, art, religion, cultural identity

Energy: Regional organization, craftsmanship, abstract thought, complex expression.

Time Period: 102,000 thousand years.

Definition: Regional consciousness spans a 102,000 year period where there is a development of complex, oral languages, the appearance of art, religions, and regional cultures. The comparative time of this evolution started in 100,000 B.C.E.

With the advent of abstract thought, (art and religion), humans were beginning to connect to Source in a rudimentary way. The cultural aspect of this time is a contrasting of one region to another and a self description from that comparison.

If this card appears in your reading, it suggests that there is no definition that can contain you. You are not your culture or religion. This card is a reminder that through art and writing, one can access a greater reality that will serve the soul's evolutionary process. Work on self expression an authenticity.

NATIONAL
6 Underworld

Key: Written language, complex buildings, sciences, national identity.

Energy: Nation organization, refinement, complex concepts, building.

Time Period: 5,125 years.

Definition: National consciousness spans a 5,125-year period. The advent of the space program, diminishing global resources, and issues with our sun have given us, as a species, a more global perspective.

Although this period of evolution required a refinement of written language, the development of science, major construction of cities, and concepts, we are required to outgrow those definitions as well. The creation of the national identity came at a time when the planet was faced with the expansive idea, that what affects one, affects all.

As with global warming or economic situations, we are part of a larger global community to the extent that unilateral decision on the environment or economy cannot be made without strengthening or toppling other, smaller nations. Consequently, with the advent of such energies, each individual must realize that each stone cast lands in a vast ocean that causes ripples throughout the universe.

If you have pulled this card in a reading, endeavor to leave behind the definitions of self, in relationship to limitations of cultures. Feel the freedom of no identity and embrace all possibilities.

GLOBAL
7 Underworld

Key: Materialism, industrialism, military complex, corporations, consumption, world government, and wars; planetary identity.

Energy: Global organization, international, production, and consumption; living in cities, technology.

Time Period: 256 years.

Definition: The Seventh Underworld, a time span of 256 years, starting in 1755, was the advent of materialism, industrialism, Americanism, democracy, and republics.

During this time of industrialization, we lost our connection with Mother Earth, became more materialistic and more focused on production of material goods than quality of life and connection to the cosmos. This is the cycle, according to the Maya, where we organized ourselves into planetary idea. If you pulled this card in your reading, it could indicate that you are relying too much on your material environment for a sense of purpose, safety, and well being. It is important to begin the paradigm shift into identifying with eternal ideas, of which you are one. It is time to reconnect with Source as your purpose and safety.

GALACTIC
8 Underworld

Key: Information, genetic, and quantum physics technology; intuition vs. scientific; global politics and wars.

Energy: Galaxy organization, dualism, revolution/ evolution, intuitive, conflict, wholeness.

Time Period: 12.8 years.

Definition: This period began in 1999 A.D. and will last 12.8 years or until December 21, 2012. According to the Maya and our own scientists, this cycle has been about moving beyond the material parameters of our existence. It is a period of accelerated "perceived" time as events and energetic frequencies increase exponentially.

During this time we are discovering that no language, short of quantum physics, can explain the constructs of energy and light that we have perceived as physical reality. It is a time of unwinding the genetic code and discovering that spirit, does indeed inform matter.

As beneficiaries of the electro-technology developed in the Seventh Underworld, we are now realizing that Grandmother Spider actually does spin an etheric web throughout the cosmos. It accommodates our cell phones, internet exchanges, and facilitates us "seeing" through our intuition, not only the past, but the future and parallel universes-and into the void, where all things and ideas are created.

If you find this Eighth Underworld card in your spread, it is a good indication that you have evolved to a point where you are ready for the shift from physicality to spiritual reality. Stay on your path and know that you are not different or separate from any other entity in the Universe. Share what you have and do not worry for what you don't have, you can create it.

UNIVERSAL
9 Underworld

Key: Unity, evolution, transcendence, transformation, end of dualism.

Energy: Polarity, awakening, reunion.

Time Period: 260 days.

Definition: This cycle began March 9, 2011 and lasted a mere 260 days; just like the gestation period for a human infant. This was the shift that many of us were waiting, dreading, and hoping for. It was a reunion with Creator, an evolutionary step that culminated an awakening over a 16.4 billion-year of time. It began with the explosion of cosmic energy that brought us into existence.

According to the Maya, the nine deities are now returned to Earth and resonating within each of us. Like a tuning fork, we are vibrating at a full-harmonic frequency, in tune with the cosmos. We are one with Creator and as such, able to give up all of the limitations that defined us as separate: from the stars, from God, from each other.

If you pulled this card, realize that you ARE the force of Creator no longer subject to limitations.

During this time, we are discovering that no language, short of quantum physics, can explain the constructs of energy and light that we have perceived as physical reality. It is a time of unwinding the genetic code and discovering that spirit does indeed inform matter.

~ Artwork and quote by Patricia A. Padilla

Chapter 7

The Four Directions

North, MULUC
South, CAUAC
East, KAN
West, IX

When we consider the importance of the four directions from the perspective of the Maya, we must give up notions of geographical location or physical attributes. Just like their ball courts, farms, or hearth sites within their homes, the Maya fashioned these to reflect the structure of the universe. The four directions connote "winds" of energy generated by the World Tree. The World Tree, or place of creation located at the galactic center, is an energetic flow of energy that holds universes together within the great void. And as the World Tree is the center point of creation, the four directions are the winds generated by the world tree and inseparable from it.[1]

The World Tree joins the thirteen Overworlds, the earth, and the nine Underworlds together within our own solar system and joins us to other universes as well.

In Maya mythology, there are the Bacabs, or deities, that are the "patrons of the beekeepers."[2] It is on the shoulders of these gods that the corners of the heavens and underworlds are supported creating a space for the earth plane. Again, it is not a geographical view but a cosmological overview of our place in the universe.

According to Quiche Maya cosmology, there is a Black Road in the sky known as Xibalba be, the road to the Underworld found at the crossing point of the Milky Way in Sagittarius. This area is known as the dark rift, or the birthing place of the stars. Extending south from the ecliptic in Sagittarius is the sac be, or White Road. Extending east and west along the ecliptic on either side of the Milky Way are the Red and Green Roads of the Maya.

Although there are variances between the Aztecs and differing tribes within the Maya culture, about the color texture and flavor of each of the four directions, it is important to understand in the reading of the cards that the influences are of a universal nature and less geophysical or political than we would assume. The Mesoamericans synchronized every aspect of their lives by the movement of the stars in the heavens. They are not separate from the universal seasons and winds; nor are we.

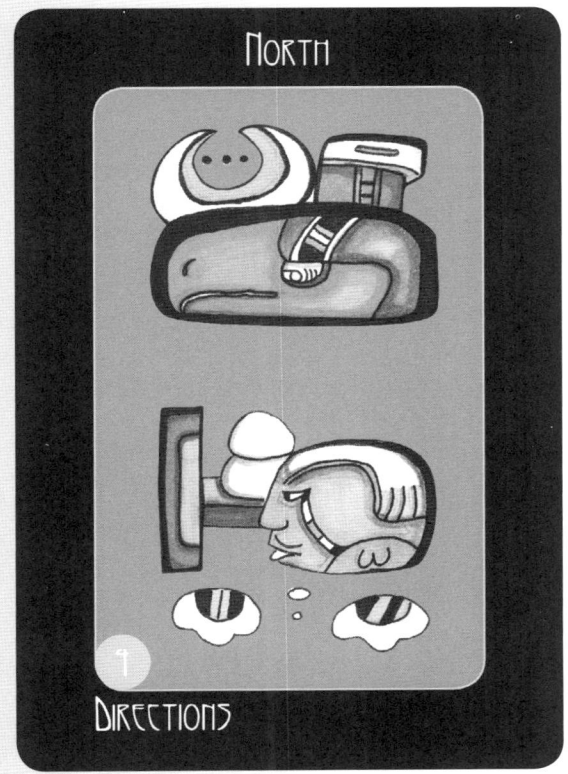

MULUC
NORTH

Power: Adaptability.

Energy: Survival.

Challenge: Emotional entanglements.

Definition: NORTH dominates during the winter, in the northern hemisphere as the sun is pushed south. The energies are separation, sacrifice, and manifestation. The associated Day is Muluc (water); the associated color is white.

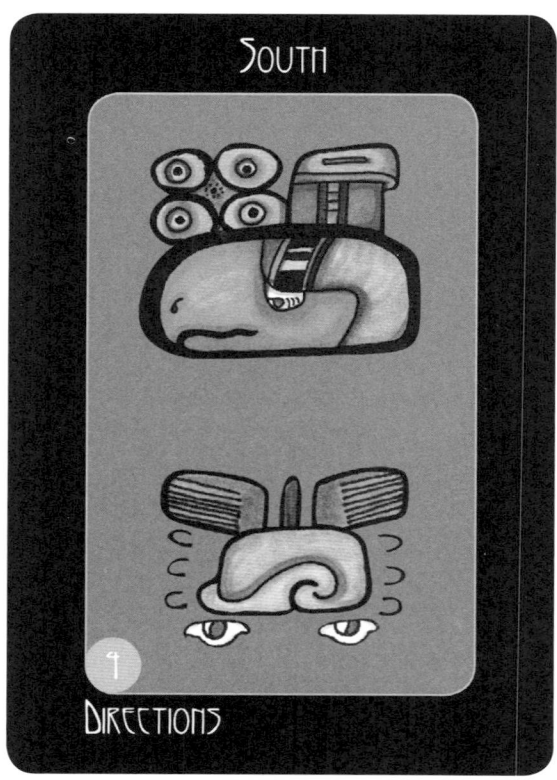

CAUAC
SOUTH

Power: Feelings/emotions.

Energy: Growth.

Challenge: Irrational thinking.

Definition: SOUTH is associated with the social and emotional life as the sun rides high in the northern sky. The energies of connection and feeling dominate. The associated Day is Cauac (storm); the associated color is red.

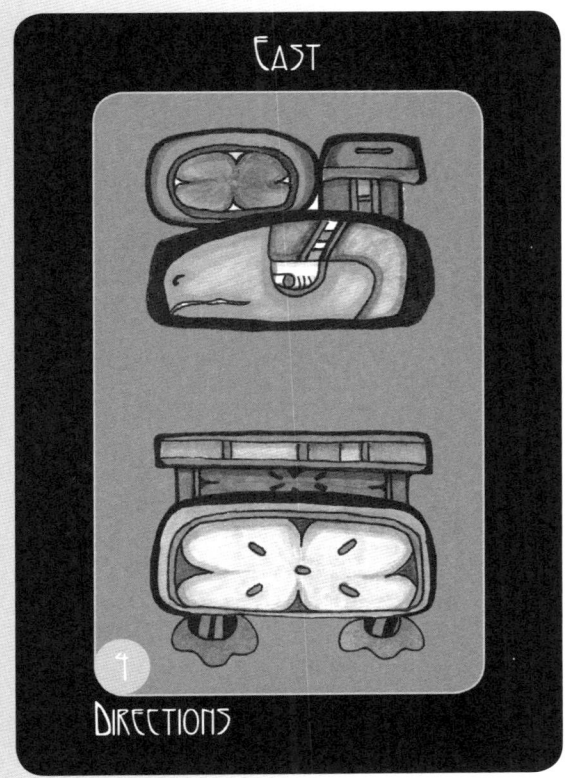

KAN
EAST

Power: New beginnings.

Energy: Self starter.

Challenge: Self-centeredness.

Definition: EAST is where the sun rises or emerges from the Underworld. It is associated with initiation and creativity. The associated Day is Kan "Corn;" the associated color is yellow.

IX
WEST

Power: Balance between two worlds (individual/collective).

Energy: Transitions.

Challenge: Indecisiveness.

Definition: WEST is where the sun merges with the Earth and descends into the Underworld. West is associated with the idea of cooperation, adjustment, and communication. The associated Day is Ix (jaguar); the associated color is black.

And when the stars are shooting above, one of our ancestors is sending us love. That's how we came to be...two stars in orbit, connected but free.

~ Aponi Kai
Artwork by Patricia A. Padilla

Chapter 8

Divine Intercession

Alchemy, Intercession
Ancestors, Intercession
Eclipse, Intercession
Hand of God, Intercession
La Reina, Intercession

Nawal, Intercession
Creation, Intercession
White Flower, Intercession
World Tree, Intercession

We have added the Intercession cards as a way of reminding ourselves that we are always held in the hand of Creator. These cards remind us that we are never alone, nor an island unto ourselves. We are born into community and exist in community. We are part of the cosmos, surrounded by the Tree People, the Rock People, the Winged Ones, the Finned Ones, and the Creepy Crawly Ones. We are affected by the stars and planets, just as the oceans and winds are; and our Ancestors are always around us.

These cards reflect the kinder side of life and give us reason to pause and wonder at who we are at any given moment in our relationship to everything. They reflect the idea that we are here to "remember" where our souls have already traveled. This is a moment to relax, breathe, and trust that the grand design is just that, Grand.

You are not alone, you are not required to be more than you already are, and there is a profound purpose in every experience.

ALCHEMY
Intercession

Power: Remember that you are the tree within the seed; let the magic happen. You are that "lily in the field," surrounded by all that you need to grow and thrive.

Definition: Looking at this Aztec design, a flower, water, and shells that adorned a carved stone box[1], one can see how nature was reflected in every part of Mesoamerican life.

Imagine how light, air, and water can manifest a rose, how a single cell splitting can create a full-grown, mature human body. Imagine how the Maya could conceive of several calendars, within calendars, and predict events 5,000 years in advance, how prayer can heal disease, or how we can change physicality with love.

The Alchemy card is to remind you of who you are: limitless, creative, and not bound by anything but your beliefs. It is an invitation to think beyond any precepts and to imagine what you would want your life to be. Open that door of possibility and be prepared to walk through. The assistance is there. It could be spiritual help and support, or come in physical form.

Insight: When this card appears in your reading, it is a reminder that all things are possible. The only challenges to your progress are the thought forms you have created around your goal.

It is a reminder to entertain more thoughts on limitless possibility and what does work for you, rather than limitations.

As we consider(ed) what the "2012 Shift"[3] is all about, it is imperative to recognize that our journey back to source is about breaking all of the barriers that have kept us from our connection with Creator. The chrysalis that encases the butterfly larvae is dissolving; let your wings expand, and prepare to take flight. This has already been written in the stars.

ANCESTORS
Intercession

Power: The idea of sacrifice and nurturing the unending cycle of birth, death, and rebirth.

Definition: A central theme prevalent to Maya cosmology is the victory of the ancestors over death, decay, and disease. Throughout Maya creation stories and rituals, there are the sacrifices that are made to sustain the circular nature of existence. The ball game is a re-enactment of the creation/ destruction/ recreation story as rituals honoring the World Tree.[3]

The ancient Maya considered the image of a turtle to represent Earth. For the Quiché Maya, the making of the Earth was similar to the creation of a maize field, which was a preparation for the human race, or people of corn. The Maya, of the modern Sierra Nahuatl of Puebla, interpret this image as people being planted like corn upon the surface of the Earth.[4] For them, we come from earth and return to earth just as the fruit and flowers do.

All of the Maya factions believe that people were formed of maize, and in the image of ancestors. The idea of sacrifice and nurturing the unending cycle of birth, death, and rebirth is a central theme.[5]

The Popol Vuh, the Maya story of creation, tells of the creator gods making humans so that they would have intelligent beings to nurture and communicate with. The shamans and priests were the select few who would go into trance, communicate with the gods and ancestors, and return with guidance and instructions on political issues and how to live. In this way, the ancestors were an integral ongoing force in Maya communities. These directives and communications were carved in stone and written by the "seers" as divine revelation from the otherworld.[6]

In the K'iché lineage shrines, a priest or shaman would conduct ceremonies on sacred days in special caves where ancestors were welcomed to commune with those that sustained them with prayer and ritual. In these caves, the afterbirth of Maya children was buried so that the ancestors would have direct connection to the ongoing generations. Priests would also receive pregnant woman and implant the woman's womb with the soul of an ancestor who was ready to return to Earth.[7]

Insight: Just as the sun rises and sets, traveling the road of Xibalba, we do, too. We come to Earth for a short time and experience physical death, to be reborn again. Just like the sun, we return to learn yet another set of lessons that will allow for our evolution. Look beyond the sleeping place of death to see infinity.

ECLIPSE
Intercession

Power: Disruption of old patterns can herald positive or negative changes.

Definition: The ancient Mayans could predict lunar and solar eclipses and viewed the celestial activity as dangerous because it was disrupting the sun's continual influence on Earth.

They often portrayed the activity as the sun and moon fighting, or ants eating the sun.[8] In this depiction of an eclipse, you can see the sky band, the glyph for the eclipse and the sky serpent preparing to devour the symbol.[9]

The Aztec people believed that unless offerings were made, the sun would not return and the Tzitzimime (star demons of darkness) would be unleashed on Earth to eat all of humanity. The ancient Maya would beat drums and play loud music; they would yell and scream to scare away the Tzitzimime from the Earth plane.[10]

Pregnant women were kept indoors and protected during eclipses to insure that the unborn children would be safe from any evil influences.[11]

In Western astrology, eclipses are known as a time when political upheavals are likely to occur and sudden shifts can happen within the Earth's atmosphere that can be positive or disruptive.

According to John Major Jenkins, an independent ancient Mesoamerican cosmology researcher, the solar eclipse on May 20, 2012, in Maya time was 10 Chicchan. Chicchan means serpent. This began a 200-year cycle for the sun-Pleiades-zenith alignment, which is said to herald the return of Quetzalcoatl as ruler of the Heart of Heaven.[12] This also coincides with the return of Christ and the dawning of a Golden age of transformation and enlightenment.[13]

The significance of the eclipse on May 20, 2012 is linked with the pyramid at Chichén Itzá where the "pyramid itself," according to Jenkins, "is a world age calendar set in stone" and points to a unique alignment in the Great cycles of precession. The pyramid is also known as the Temple of Kukulcan, which is the Maya name for Quetzalcoatl. On any equinox, Kukulcan (Quetzalcoatl) manifests on the nine-level structure and slithers down the stairs as the cosmic alignment occurs on the equinox. What is interesting is, on the May 2012 date, this initiates a new era.[14] Could it be that the return of Quetzalcoatl, during this important eclipse date, was what has been prophesied for so long?

Insight: For our purposes, we see this important eclipse date as yet another sign for the advent of a new age of enlightenment and peace.

HAND OF GOD
Intercession

Power: This depiction of the hand of Creator is to remind us that we truly do reside in the palm of the hand of Creator. All we have to do is remain aware of who, where, and what we are; to enter into the flow of Creator's will.

Definition: If the Maya left us with anything, it is the idea that we are functioning and evolving within a grand design. The prophecies of the Maya, allow us to know, that there is a Divine progression that has been "written in the stars."

As in many other world traditions, the signature hand of God can indicate intervention, a blessing, or the suggestion that we do indeed reside in the hand of Creator.

The most recent depiction of the Hand of God comes from the cosmos, captured by NASA's Chandra Observatory. It is a spinning neutron star, or pulsar that is releasing energy as it rotates. The resulting pattern is the image of a huge hand in the heavens that is 12 miles in diameter and is producing a cloud 150 light years across space.[15] It is a sign of the times.

This image of the Hand of God, like every other star, planet, or constellation, is just another reminder that we are all in process, a part of a greater design that was initiated outside of a time frame and beyond any construct we can imagine. Perhaps that is what this evolutionary period is all about... reclaiming that memory of our true identity and purpose.

Insight: This card in a reading would indicate that there is no need for correction or control; it is in God's hands.

LA REINA
Intercession

Power: "I wish that a temple be erected here quickly, so I may therein exhibit and give all my love, compassion, help, and protection. Because I am your merciful mother, to you, and to all the inhabitants on this land and all the rest who love me, invoke and confide in me; to listen there to their lamentations, and remedy all their miseries, afflictions, and sorrows."

~Words of Our Lady to Juan Diego
(Nican Mopohua)

Definition: This depiction of Nuestra Senora de Guadalupe, or Our Lady of Guadalupe, is an interpretation from the image at The Basilica in Mexico City.

Legend has it that, in the 1500s, a peasant man named Juan Diego was traveling from a small village in the mountains to Mexico City to ask the Catholic Bishop to come and bless a dying relative. On the journey, he saw an apparition of the Blessed Mother.

She asked Juan to petition the Bishop to build a cathedral in her honor in Mexico City. Although the Bishop could easily dismiss the story and the request as though it had come from a man with an over-active imagination, he could not help but notice the imprint of the Blessed Mother which rested silently under an apron full of roses that Diego delivered as a "sign" of her presence.

The Blessed Mother (of Jesus), told Diego that she was the embodiment of all of the gods of the Maya and Aztecs and that the native people of Mexico would not be forsaken. She is always there to guard and protect them from any darkness or evil.

The Bishop knew that under mundane circumstances, roses would not bloom in the snowy mountains of Tepayac, in the middle of winter, and took the request seriously.

Today, the Basilica is a destination spot for pilgrims from every country, faith, and age group. It is a place where people go expecting miracles.

Insight: No matter what you call your god, there is Divinity that upholds and surrounds you. Love is eternal, it can be referred to in many ways, but it is always Love, the "glue" that holds the universe in place.

NAWAL
Intercession

Power: Nawals are animal spirit protectors, informants, and always walk with us through this life.

Definition: For the Maya, the soul is a complex idea. There is the eternal and indestructible soul and a "chanul" or "nawal."[16] This is a supernatural guardian spirit or protector that comes as an animal spirit and shares the journey of life with a child from birth. The life path of both souls is intertwined. What occurs with one occurs with the other. It can be likened to "spirit guide" in New Age circles or a totem in Native American tribes.

The nawal, or animal spirit, that accompanies the Maya children, are taken care of by the ancestral Father-Mother creator gods. These guardian spirits are kept in a magical corral inside of the mountains until a child is born.[17]

It the gods get angry, they can affect the fate of a child by refusing to nurture and care for the nawal of that person. This can inspire the parents to keep peace with the gods and perform rituals with sincerity and purpose.[18]

Individuals can become acquainted with their nawal through shamanic healings or dreams, sometimes through bloodletting or during a curing ceremony performed by a shaman.

As we care for ourselves, we also must care for the animal spirit that accompanies us on our life path, protecting it as we protect ourselves. In every instance of Mesoamerican cosmology, the interconnection between physicality and spirit is emphasized. We cannot be healthy physically without nurturing the spirit and spirit helpers that accompany us.

Within the western idea, it has become more acceptable to seek out and become acquainted with these "guides" as we attempt to cure physical, mental, or emotional illnesses. The advent of mind/body therapies have prompted us to try to catch up with the ancient ones.

Insight: As you care for yourself or others, know that you are engaging a nawal, a spirit guardian from another dimension that is there to serve and protect you. This unseen help is ever your advocate.

CREATION
Intercession

Power: Life returns to earth in the form of germinating maize; all creation waxes and wanes in creative cycles.

Definition: The Creation card is inspired by an image from the Madrid Codex. The turtle is shown suspended from cords attached to the skyband, because Orion hangs below the ecliptic. The ecliptic is the path traveled by the sun, moon, and stars through the sky. Twelve constellations lie along the ecliptic course where the sun progresses through each "house," within a solar year. You may be familiar with the terms, if you are versed in astrology.

As anthropologists have come to learn, Maya art is all about our connection to the cosmos. In this drawing, Linda Schele, the late Mayanist scholar, identified the picture as Orion the turtle. It was from the cracked carapace of the turtle shell that the maize god emerged. The three stones on the turtles back, in this drawing, are the three stars in the belt of Orion. These are mirrored in the hearth stones of traditional Maya homes and have the significance of the "three stones of Creation."[19] This is where First Father comes from and the idea of lightning and fire heralding the beginning of time. According to Carl Johan Calleman, First Father is also the Maize God, so the celestial movement of the sun past the Orion-Gemini constellations, in June, evokes the annual rebirth of life-giving maize. Life returns to earth in the form of germinating maize.

Linda Schele, Maya Cosmos, viewed this configuration as a "cosmic navel of creation," the place in Gemini, where the Milky Way crosses the ecliptic, forming the cosmic axis or trunk of the World Tree. This axis point for the Maya was the Place of Creation and rebirth.[20]

Insight: For our purposes, we chose this image to represent our own experiences of the waxing and waning of creativity. We celebrate the cyclical nature of the Universe and again, are no different from the stars and planets, from our own Earth and her regeneration. It is so with creativity as well. We have periods of intense insights and times of rest and regeneration. Be patient with yourself as you allow your creative consciousness to rest and regenerate.

WHITE FLOWER
Intercession

Power: The flower of the World Tree is the eternal indestructible soul of each of us.

Definition: White Flower Tree is another representation of the World Tree seen replicated throughout Maya world. It is the earthly recreation of the Cosmic Tree seen in the heavens. The World Tree, Cosmic Tree, Wakah-Chan, or the crosses that you see throughout Mesoamerica, are all representational of the "place of creation," next to Orion in the heavens.[21]

The white flowers depicted on the tree are the portal way where souls of human beings are brought to Earth. As the flowers bloom, the eternal, indestructible soul of each human is brought forth to the Earth to live, yet again.

The Maya sing to this tree and feed the tree in order to sustain the proliferation of human souls.[22] Flowers are the holy representation of human souls. The flower is the eternal, indestructible soul of each of us.

In the tradition of the Maya of Palenque, when the owner of the soul dies, it hangs around the grave for awhile before it goes back to a pool of souls. K'an-Hub-Matawil or "Precious-

Shell-Matawil" is where First Mother and First Father, the ancestral parents and the children reside. The keeper of the white-flower souls takes them to dwell there, until the gods place them in the womb of a new mother.[23]

Insight: As we progress through our thirteen stages of germination to full adulthood and death, we are escorted with guides and guardians that strive to keep us in harmony with Creator. We are never alone or without help.

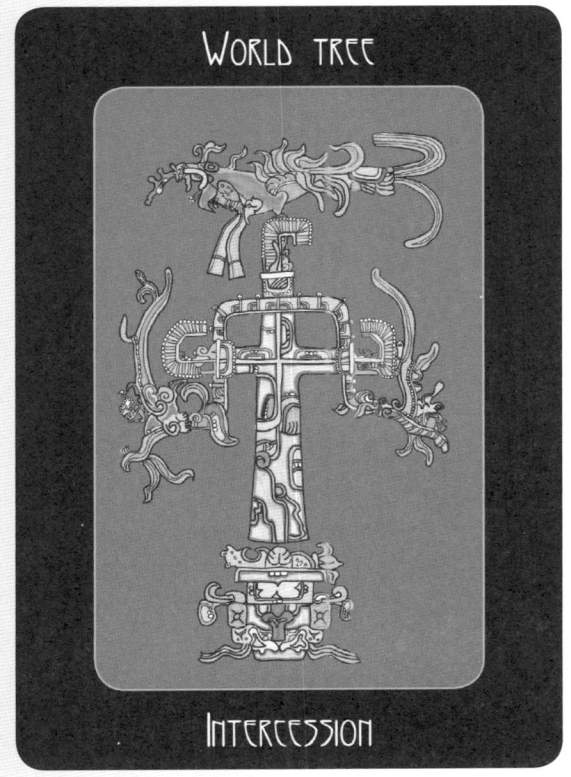

WORLD TREE
Intercession

Power: "…The elders say we must let go of the shore, and push off and into the river, keep our eyes open, and our head above the water. See who is in the river with you, and Celebrate… At this time in history, we are to take nothing personally. Least of all ourselves. For the moment that we do, our spiritual growth and journey comes to a halt… WE ARE THE ONES WE'VE BEEN WAITING FOR…"

~Hopi Nation Oraibi
Arizona September, 2001

Definition: If you are fortunate enough to stand beneath a moonless, cloudless night sky and see the exquisite formation of the Milky Way, you cannot miss the main signs along the Star Road. These star patterns were the cosmic road map for the Maya.

These same patterns defined Maya culture in every aspect, from birth to war to what to eat on any given day. The organization of the heavens determined how to build their homes, play ball games, and give birth.

In the center of the Star Road (Milky Way) one can identify the World Tree. It is not only the World Tree of the Maya, but of most indigenous people. In Maya culture, the World Tree is the common thread that holds the 13 Overworlds, 9 Underworlds, and Earth plane together.[24]

This cosmological construct, emanating from the heavens, creates the four directions. Each direction has its own frequency and generates its own "spiritual wind."[25]

This replication in The Star Road Map deck is a replication of the Foliated Cross from Palenque. There is a detailed creation story in all of the symbols, but the cross itself is a replica of the World Tree that is the beginning place of all life.[26]

The World Tree, wherever it appears, is often referred to as "raised-up-sky-place" and comes from a time when the Earth was flooded and four gods were assigned to uphold the heavens to prevent a collapse of the sky in to the oceans. Throughout Mesoamerica, one can see green crosses that appear in every village. These are not the Christian icons that one would suspect; they are ancient replicas of the original World Tree. Often they will be decorated with pine boughs and flowers and there will be offerings close to the cross structures. Their belief is that to sustain the ever-present World Tree, where all of life comes from, is to sustain life here on Earth.[27]

According to Carl Johan Calleman, the World Tree is the "tuning fork" of evolution. If you imagine its span throughout the Underworlds and Overworlds, each epoch an awakening of consciousness, then the Overworlds and Underworlds becoming "activated" makes sense.

We are tuning up, turning on, and evolving into Hunab K'u's completed creation. The pivotal 2012 date signifies the completion of the evolution of the human or the completion of the evolutionary progression of the ninth Underworld, (which is the description of the evolution of the human brain). What will the next epoch be?

Insight: For the past 16.5 billion years, a plan of evolution has been described by the Maya, in their calendar system, outlining the evolution of the human race. Their information, stunningly accurate, reassures us that Hunab K'u is, and has always been, in charge. Our insight into the changes taking place now, "is to let go and let God." Relax, ride the wave, and be open to your own expansion.

Perhaps the most important relationship that we can focus on is with self. It is only through this endeavor that we connect with Creator. This is where we encounter the part of us that is eternal, non-diminished by physical circumstance, and the reservoir of wisdom inherent within all of us.

~Patricia A. Padilla

Chapter 9

Hall of Mirrors

Have you ever visited the House of Mirrors at a theme park or carnival and walked away in hysterical laughter for all the ridiculous, desirable, and not so desirable images cast back at you from the different shaped mirrors? It is disorienting, for sure; but interesting. We leave there, wondering which image most closely resembles who we are in the world or just who we are.

Life is a hall of mirrors. Everything that we believe or think or suspect is reflected back to us through the people and situations we encounter. It is as if we are the projectors and the world-at-large is our screen. There is a vast amount of distance, noise, and confusion between our conscious and subconscious mind. Let's be honest, we in the western hemisphere are not trained, nor encouraged, to develop self knowledge.

For many, the conscious mind rules; that is the area of the five senses, of logic, deductive reasoning— rules and regulations. The five senses—touch, sight, smell, vision, and hearing—orient us in the physical world.

As the conscious mind acts as a filter for the relentless assault of incoming information, the subconscious mind registers every minute detail of our environment. The conscious filter (or conscious mind) insures the survival of our physical body. The unconscious mind registers everything from precognition, clairvoyance, clairsentience, prescience, and our greater connection to all that is.

Often, we never consider our subconscious mind until our world is shattered by trauma or loss. Consider the veterans who come back from the war zone and cannot acclimate to the society they left, or the child who loses his mother at a young age and never stops looking for her in every female he/she encounters. These life circumstances are too raw and painful to bring with us to our day-to-day existence, so we suppress or deny or bury our fears and emotions far beneath the surface of what is socially acceptable.

Whether we want to own the experiences or not, the body remembers and the subconscious mind will symbolically present the unresolved issues until we pay attention and work to restore balance within ourselves. We may experience the unresolved issues in dreams or see the issue played out before us, over and over again until we stop the chaos and begin excavation into our subconscious mind.

We exist in relationship. We are in relation with the Earth and the moon and stars, to each other, the animal kingdom, and the sea creatures. We even have relationships with bugs and plants.

As we evolve through this lifetime, from relationship to relationship, we are often confused by what we want, what we get, and how to get what we want. Oftentimes, we want the very things that cause us the most grief. Confusion is often created when our subconscious mind is in conflict with our conscious mind and we feel stuck, not knowing how to create flow and balance.

Perhaps the most important relationship that we can focus on is with self. It is only through this endeavor that we connect with Creator. This is where we encounter the part of us that is eternal, non-diminished by physical circumstance, and the reservoir of wisdom inherent within all of us.

When we open the portals of communication between our conscious and subconscious mind, our efforts to sustain our physical, emotional, spiritual, and mental objectives are much clearer and more likely to take form.

The doorway between these two realms of consciousness is where we meet God face to face. It is the entry point for creativity, inspiration, and compassion.

One way to work on inner and outer harmony is to initiate a dialogue with ourselves and indeed the universe, through the language of symbols. As Carl Jung said, "the psychological mechanism for transforming energy is the symbol." Just as it has been said that mathematics is the language of God, (the Mayans certainly seemed to believe this), archetypes and symbols are just another set of signs that are employed to ferret out an ultimate truth within this eternal moment. Like every other Tarot deck, The Star Road Map deck uses the same archetypal ideas, such as the Emperor, Empress, Sun, and Moon, etc. The archetypes are symbols or images that carry the same meaning across cultures and languages. They are symbols of our human experience and relationship to self, others, and the universe at large.

The difference in this deck is the world view. Instead of having four suits, we have the 22 archetypical images, the 9 Underworlds (the stages of development of the human brain); the 13 Overworlds (the evolutionary, spiritual influences from Creator to stimulate an evolutionary process), and the Day signs, to allow one to consider what energy is assisting growth and awareness.

Allow yourself to contemplate the images and information that you draw forth. Wonder at the synchronicity of the symbols and how they interact with the current issues in your life. These signs will serve as mirrors of your internal labyrinth and can act as inspiration or warning, as you travel the Star Road.

Chapter 10

Reading the Map

One-Card Reading
Three-Card Reading
Six-Card Reading
Full Reading Using All 78 Cards

God speaks to us in symbols. For whatever language we speak, even if it is a few different languages, it is still true that "a picture is worth a thousand words." Pictures can only be interpreted by your soul. A picture can evoke feelings and connect us to memories that expand or contract us.

Archetypes, pictures of Earth for instance, say so much more than that she sustains us, that we grow our food and families on her, and that her moods and seasons affect our way of living. We also can glean from a photo or a depiction that she is a unit of a greater whole and the image can suggest that she has a place in a larger universe. In a symbol of Mother Earth, we can wonder at our relationship to her and her fragility or resilience. Whereas, if we hear the word "earth," we relate the context of the word to the rest of the sentence or idea.

As you discover *The Star Road Map* symbols, let the images speak to you. They are ancient symbols for the same ideas that we live with today. As you draw a card for contemplation, sit with the image. Contemplate what this image is evoking in you and study the meaning for how it applies to you in the moment or as an overall energy of your existence.

One-Card Reading

There is also a very effective, short meditation that is a great way to familiarize your self with the cards.
Draw one card to contemplate for the day. Observe how it applies to current concerns or how it directs you to deal with an issue you have been thinking about.

It may be that the idea that is presented will be an issue or circumstance that you deal with in the course of the day.

Example

I have a relationship that is troubling me. There has been no communication and the images and feelings surrounding the issue cause me grief.

Card pulled: World Tree

The meaning of this card is that the World Tree is an earthly image, reminding us, that we are part of a much larger reality. The World Tree is a centering of ourselves in the Universe.

Like a "tuning fork," all of the 16.4 billion years of evolution have been about attuning to the cosmos, by the evolutionary process designed by Creator.

This would suggest that the only way to resolve this feeling of "unfinished business" is to see the entire relationship as a process of evolving beyond personality and personal desire to the realization that the lesson of this relationship is part of a much larger lesson, and not about them or me. The meaning of this card, in short, is "to let go and let God."

The fact that I pulled an intercession card would indicate that it is not up to me to complete this understanding but something that is being negotiated by Spirit, to foster a deeper evolutionary process within myself.

In short, let go!

Three-Card Reading

A meditation might be to draw three cards for what energies you should be aware of in the moment.

Cards pulled:
21 Self Love, 02 Priestess, and 6 Day.

Example

I am asking the cards to show me what I should consider as I finish this Tarot deck. I am mindful of representing an ancient culture and honor the world view of the ancestors.

21 Self Love Card.

Goal: To walk in beauty, think in beauty and act in beauty.

The story of Xochiquetzal is a tragic one. Like Eve, in the Garden of Eden, she looks for beauty and sustenance outside of herself and adorns herself, and eats, from the forbidden tree. Having gone against the orders of Ometeotl (the Supreme Being), she was cast out into a barren desert and her sight was taken away. Now she is the bringer of beauty because she realizes that it is internal, not external.

02 Priestess Card.

Goal: Step aside and humbly ask for guidance. Beneath what appears as chaos and confusion, is often a brilliant truth that can further the soul's understanding.

The Priestess is able to traverse universes by stepping outside of the conscious mind and shackles of the five senses. She avails herself to Creator by stopping her thought process and becoming an open channel for cosmic/divine energy.

This can be accomplished by meditation, prayer, yoga, tai chi, or the bloodletting, of old. My recommendation is meditation, the process of stopping conscious thought and connecting with infinite mind.

6 Day Card.

Energy: Security, conscious, materialistic, tradition.

Challenge: Avoid being a victim and don't sacrifice too much to make others happy; develop your natural inclination.

Solution: Make your efforts count; become useful to society and the world at large.

As I review the cards drawn in relation to the question, I am aware that from the first card drawn,
Self Love, that I must trust myself and know that what I am moved to say about these images is enough. I do not need to study and peruse other texts in order to validate what the image or meaning inspires for this text.

The second card, the Priestess, validates that the connection to what needs to be shared, is within. Trust it. If I question the direction, I will go into meditation and allow the direction to clarify.

The 6 Day card validates for me that, indeed, there is a connection with the ancient tradition I am writing about.

Overall, I would say that the spread is a validation that what has been put together honors all of my promptings for this deck.

Six-Card Reading

Draw three cards, place side by side.

Draw three more cards, place on top of first three; this compromises one issue facing you in this moment. Read the six cards as one idea.

This reading has to do with the Gulf of Mexico oil spill (2010) and identifies the lesson:

Cards pulled:
20 Day, 7 Underworld, 03 Empress, 17 Moon, 1 Overworld, and Creation

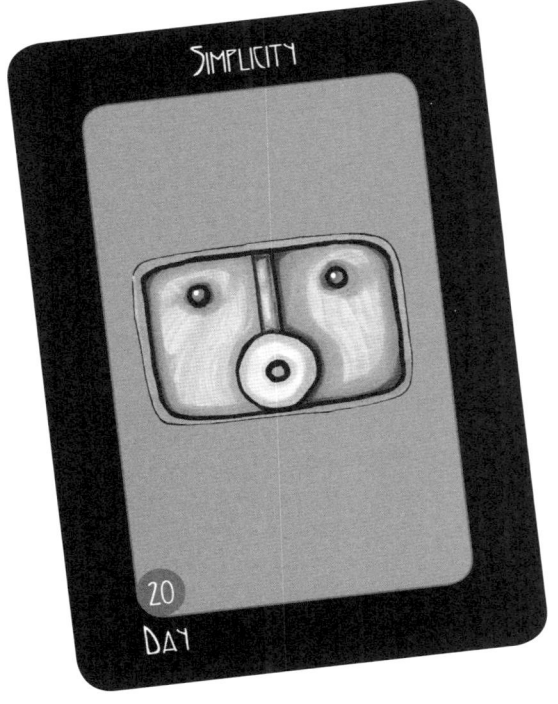

20 Day Card.

South: Simplicity.
Key words: idealistic, artistic, romantic, dreamy, Radiant Sun God, religion, and art.

Challenge: Learn to handle disappointments due to unrealistic expectations and to tolerate unfairness in others.

Solution: Simplicity in all things, in heaven and on Earth.

7 Underworld Card.

Planetary.

Key words: Materialism, industrialism, consumption, and global identity.

During this time of industrialization we lost our connection to Mother Earth. We became more materialistic and more focused on production of material goods than quality of life and connection to the cosmos.

"If you pulled this card in your reading, it could indicate that you are relying too much on your material environment for a sense of purpose, safety, and well being. It is important to begin the paradigm shift into identifying with eternal ideas, of which you are one. It is time to reconnect with Source as your purpose and safety."

03 Empress Card.

Compassion.

Energetic: The Empress card represents the earthly mother as a replica of the great goddess.

Goal: If this card appears in your reading, it is a signal to look at the situation with the wisdom and compassion of the Empress. Serving as a conduit for compassion and selflessness, can and will advance your efforts in any situation. When we love in this manner we remove ourselves as targets of misunderstanding.

(From the history portion of the image)
"She also protected humanity by changing people into fish, so that the waters would not drown them; and by creating a bridge linking Earth to heaven for those in her favor."

Shadow: Think of the failed opportunities to love and understand and you may have a good idea of how a situation can go wrong.

17 Moon Card.

Key: Embracing the shadow.

Energetic: It is generally considered that this card represents our deepest unidentified desires and fears.

This card can also represent lunacy and the 28-day cycle of the moon as it orbits Earth.

Goal: The moon can affirm that we are intimate with self, that we acknowledge what is real and what is fantasy.

Inspiration: As the moon orbits the Earth and disappears to the underworld, we also cycle into our own death and rebirth with every moon rise and set. This is a journey between the veil of life and death and rebirth. We come back with a deeper understanding of what it is to be human; to change and grow, to suffer and recover.

Light: This card could indicate that we have done the work necessary to allow our intuitive instincts to guide us.

Shadow: In a poor placement can indicate delusion, drug abuse, fear, and a sojourn into the dark night of the soul with no tools or skills to re-emerge.

1 Overworld Card.

Initiation.

Positive Aspect: This card in a spread could indicate a strong and grand beginning to a project or relationship or idea. We have in place, all we need to blossom and thrive.

Negative Aspect: Hun (the name of the card) can be an impediment rather than a thrust towards completion. Don't get too mental or try to recreate creation. In short, get out of the way and let Divine intelligence lead. If you are already in a new relationship, business venture or project, it could necessitate starting again from the beginning and let the inherent flow that is already present, guide you.

Xiuhtecuhtli was the Lord of volcanoes and the personification of life after death. He was the god of fire, day, and heat; warmth and cold, light and darkness, and food during famine.

He is also known as the "Turquoise Lord," or "Lord of Fire." A sacred fire was always kept burning in the temples of Xiuhtecuhtli in gratitude for the gift of fire; the first mouthful from each meal was flung into the hearth.

Creation Card.

As anthropologists have come to learn, Maya Art is all about our connection to the cosmos. The three stones on the turtles back are the three stars in the belt of Orion. These are mirrored in the hearth stones of traditional Maya homes and have the significance of the three stones of creation. This is where first father comes from and the idea of lightening and fire heralding the beginning of time.

Insight: For our purposes, we choose this image to represent our own experiences of the waxing and waning of creativity. We celebrate the cyclical nature of the universe and again, are no different than the stars and planets or our own Earth and regenerative processes.

It is so with creativity as well. We have periods of intense insights and times of rest and regeneration.

In an overall analysis of this six-card spread, representing one idea, I will look at how one card justifies another and deepens the meaning of just a six-card spread. Remember, the question is: What do we need to learn from this calamity?

Card 20 Day with the meaning of simplicity and the keywords of artistic, romantic, and dreamy would indicate that denial is operative, around the damage and destruction of the Gulf oil spill. The fact that 20 Day is affiliated with the direction of the South is interesting. Since the primary meaning of this card is simplicity. I believe this is a warning to simplify our lives and the cleanup effort. It doesn't mean to NOT make such an effort, but to look to naturally occurring elements to restore balance to the challenged waters. This reading would definitely not support a nuclear explosion to deal with the gusher!

Looking straight across to the right, in the top three-card spread, we see 7 Underworld, which is the card that signifies a planetary concern, and in its deeper meaning, talks to us of our evolutionary stage of materialism, greed, and loss of connection to the Earth and the cosmos. That is certainly how we got into this dilemma. If you compare simplicity with materialism, it doesn't look good.

The third card in the top row, to the right again, is the Empress, offering a suggestion about how to deal with the situation. She represents the Earth, compassion, and love, understanding and a willingness to give and do what is necessary for her children and loved ones to survive.

On the second row, we have Moon on top of 20 Day (keywords: simplicity, dreamy). This configuration would suggest that the dreaminess under the Moon card is a strong denial or lunacy around what is taking place. The threat is to be submerged in the denial which could cause us to fail to do what is necessary to survive the ordeal; it is a warning.

The second configuration is the 1 Overworld card, on top of the 7 Underworld card.

Remember, 1 Overworld is associated with initiation, with new business or relationship ventures. It could be a positive or a negative. In this case, resting on 7 Underworld (a 256 period that began in 1755), it is a step backward in our evolution. Here, we go back to planetary consciousness or materialism, when we are actually at the evolutionary point in the cosmos of Galactic consciousness.

The oil drilling venture was doomed because it was initiated from a limited soul perspective of greed and materialism.

Interestingly enough, the god of the 1Overworld is Xiuhtecuhtli, (the god of fire and volcanoes). He rules over fire, lightning, heat and cold, famine and plenty. Xiuhtecuhtli is known as the "Turquoise God," which would be the color of the beautiful gulf waters, with both the warm and cold currents. I would suspect that the British Petroleum officials angered Xiuhtecuhtli and that would indicate that maybe it would have been best for them to get out of the way of the cleanup process.

The third configuration, the Empress card with the Creation card is an appropriate closure to the six-card spread. The intercession cards indicate that the "Hand of God" is at work on the issue and to "let go and let God." Creation is a replica of the belt of Orion, the beginning of father, time, lightning, and fire.

The elements of lightning and fire are elements of purification, so this reading would indicate that we are not only going through such a period but in referring back to the first card in the spread, it is necessary to return to simplicity.

...TOONEC CK'ATICTECH YUM HUNAB K'U CA A CANZAHOOB LE BEHO
We ask you, Master Hunab K'u, to show us the path.

ANTON YUM HUNAB K'U LI TIAL CA ZUTNAG LE IN LAK'ECHO
Help us, Master Hunab K'u, to regain fraternal love.

CK'ATICTECH C'YUM HUNAB K'U TIAL MA ZATAL. OH YUM HUNAB K'U!
We ask this of you, Master, Giver of Movement and Measure, so that we do not lose ourselves.
Oh Master, Hunab K'u!

~Humbatz, Men
from *Secrets of Mayan Science/Religion*

Conclusion

It appears that the Mesoamericans, so long ago, were speaking to us of a change that can only be described as a neurogenesis. Over a 16.5 million-year period, the predictions were all about the soul's growth and maturation through layers of limitation. We are no longer amoebas undulating through primordial slime; nor Neanderthals poised only for the next meal. We can no longer use technology such as nuclear powered heating without being aware of the consequences of a nuclear meltdown.

We are not just a nation or a notion of separate families, tribes, or national identities with a unique agenda for survival and wellbeing. We have expanded our consciousness to include the exploration of Mars and space stations that humans inhabit. We, as a global community, are watching our sun evolve, which is causing global changes that are transforming the way we use our medicine and how we live.

The Internet has changed our mode of communication and it is now becoming obsolete as we realize we are a phenomenon of non-local reality. We are learning to perceive truth in a new way—as the antenna that receives and transmits information. Should solar flares annihilate our satellites and stop all electronic transmissions, we will soon discover that we didn't need these physical structures; for we are one.

The Mesoamericans already understood all of this, not through physical experience, but by the interaction they had with stars and their subconscious minds. They gleaned much of their information from bloodletting and ritual, watched the movement of the planets, and had a keen observance of the natural world. Isn't it strange that the ancient wisdom is now cutting-edge science that we are scrambling to create a language to describe?

As we read about limitations being proposed for Internet access and usage by governments, it is laughable to realize that the Mesoamericans had no technology at all! No earthly force can sever you from Grand Intelligence that is the soul's arena. And it is only our self-perception, educated by a social system, that limits us.

Could it be when the Maya built their farms, hearths, and birthing rooms to align with the constellation of Orion, that they were remembering their place of origin? Was it that they were homesick for a realm that did not accept death, but saw only an evolutionary process of growth and change? I suspect the ultimate message from these ancient tribes is that we are all star seeds, not subject to ultimate annihilation, but eternally changing to reflect the perfection of Source.

Endnotes

Chapter 1

1. The date (22,000) is still under debate—that started in part with the following paper. Barney J. Szabo, Harold E. Malde and Cynthia Irwin-Williams. "Dilemma Posed by Uranium-Series Dates on Archaeologically Significant Bones from Valsequillo, Puebla, Mexico." (http://pleistocenecoalition.com/steen-mcintyre/Szabo_et_all_1969.pdf) Pg. 1
2. Jenkins, John Major. *Maya Cosmogenesis 2012*. (Rochester, VT:Bear & Company, 1998). Pg. 19
3. "Popol Vuh Relief—El Mirador, Guatemala." Zorich, Zach. Archaeology, Vol. 63 No.1 (January/February, 2010) http://archaeology.org/1001/topten/guatemala.html
4. Calleman, Carl Johan. *The Mayan Calendar and the Transformation of Consciousness*. (Rochester, VT: Bear & Company, 2004). Pg. 149-150
5. "Diego de Landa." Wikipedia, the free encyclopedia. (November 19, 2011). http://en.wikipedia.org/wiki/Diego_de_Landa
6. Ibid., 1
7. Calleman, Carl Johan. *The Mayan Calendar and the Transformation of Consciousness*. (Rochester, VT: Bear & Company, 2004). Pg. 89
8. Jenkins, John Major. *Maya Cosmogenesis 2012*. (Rochester, VT: Bear & Company, 1998). Pg. 3-65
9. Calleman, Carl Johan. *The Purposeful Universe: How Quantum Theory and Mayan Cosmology Explain the Origin and Evolution of Life*. (Rochester, VT: Bear & Company, 2009). Pg. 2-3
10. Ibid., 5-10
11. Ibid., 29, 266-67
12. "Mayan Calendar: The World Will Not End." Barrios, Carlos. Maya Mystery School (2011). www.mayamysteryschool.com
13. "Is the Sun Emitting a Mystery Particle?" O'Neil, Ian. *Discovery News* (2010). http://news.discovery.com/space/is-the-sunemitting-a-mystery-particle.html
14. "Strange Case of Solar Flares and Radioactive Elements, The." Strober, Dan. (Stanford Report, 2010.) http://news.stanford.edu/news/2010/august/sun-082310.html

Chapter 2

1. Coe, Michael D. and Rex Koontz. *Mexico: From the Olmecs to the Aztecs*. (New York, NY: Thames & Hudson Inc., 2008). Pg. 205
2. Ibid., 206
3. Phillips, Charles. *The Complete Illustrated History: Aztec & Maya*. (New York, NY: Metro Books, 2008). Pg. 375
4. "Centzon Totochtin." Wikipedia, the free encyclopedia. (November 19, 2011). http://en.wikipedia.org/wiki/Centzon_Totochtin
5. Meyer, Karl E. *Teotihuacán*. (New York, NY: Newsweek: Wonders of Man Series, 1973). Pg. 133
6. Ibid., 133
7. "Lady Xoc." Wikipedia, the free encyclopedia. (November 19, 2011). http://en.wikipedia.org/wiki/Lady_Xoc
8. Foster, Lynn V. *Handbook to Life in the Ancient Maya World*. (New York, NY: Oxford University Press, 2005). Pg. 193
9. Phillips, Charles. *The Complete Illustrated History: Aztec & Maya*. (New York, NY: Metro Books, 2008). Pg. 213
10. "Chalchiuhtlicue." Encyclopædia Britannica Online. (November 19, 2011). http://www.britannica.com/EBchecked/topic/104607/Chalchiuhtlicue
11. Phillips, Charles. The Complete Illustrated History: Aztec & Maya. (New York, NY: Metro Books, 2008). Pg. 148
12. "Chalchiuhtlicue." Encyclopædia Britannica Online. (November 19, 2011). http://www.britannica.com/EBchecked/topic/104607/Chalchiuhtlicue
13. Phillips, Charles. *The Complete Illustrated History: Aztec & Maya*. (New

York, NY: Metro Books, 2008). Pg. 172
14. Ibid., 108
15. Ibid., 108
16. Mary Miller and Karl Taube. *An Illustrated Dictionary of the Gods and Symbols of Ancient Mexico and the Maya*. (New York, NY: Thames & Hudson Inc., 1993). Pg. 164
17. Phillips, Charles. *The Complete Illustrated History: Aztec & Maya*. (New York, NY: Metro Books, 2008). Pg. 178
18. Ibid., 178
19. "Ometecuhtli." Encyclopædia Britannica Online. (November 19, 2011). http://www.britannica.com/EBchecked/topic/428358/Ometecuhtli
20. "Quetzalcoatl." Encyclopædia Britannica Online. (November 19, 2011). http://www.britannica.com/EBchecked/topic/487168/Quetzalcoatl
21. Ibid., 1
22. "Quetzalcoatl." Myths and Legends of the World. 2001. Encyclopedia.com. (November 19, 2011). www.encyclopedia.com/doc/1G2-3490900408.html
23. Mary Miller and Karl Taube. *An Illustrated Dictionary of the Gods and Symbols of Ancient Mexico and the Maya*. (New York, NY: Thames & Hudson Inc., 1993). Pg. 180
24. Carrasco, David. *Quetzalcoatl and the Irony of Empire: Myths and Prophecies in the Aztec Tradition*. (Chicago, IL: The University of Chicago Press, 1982). Pg. 174
25. "Corn Deities and the Complementary Male/Female Principle." Bassie-Sweet, Karen. Mesoweb.com. (November 9, 2011). www.mesoweb.com/features/bassie/corn/media/corn_deities.pdf. Pg. 11-13
26. Ibid., 11-13
27. Ibid., 16
28. Ibid., 17
29. Phillips, Charles. *The Complete Illustrated History: Aztec & Maya*. (New York, NY: Metro Books, 2008). Pg. 212
30. Ibid., 213
31. Ibid., 213
32. Ibid., 213
33. "Vucub Caquix." Wikipedia, the free encyclopedia. (November 19, 2011). http://en.wikipedia.org/wiki/Vucub_Caquix
34. Brennan, Martin. *The Hidden Maya: A New Understanding of Maya Glyphs*. (Rochester, VT: Bear & Company, 1998). Pg. 30
35. Gilbert, Adrian. *The Hidden Maya: A New Understanding of Maya Glyphs*. (Rochester, VT: Bear & Company, 1998). Pg. 124-27
36. Jenkins, John Major. *Maya Cosmogenesis 2012*. (Rochester, VT: Bear & Company, 1998). Pg. 258-62
37. "Tzitzimitl." Wikipedia, the free encyclopedia. (November 19, 2011). http://en.wikipedia.org/wiki/Tzitzimitl
38. Ibid., 1
39. Mary Miller and Karl Taube. *An Illustrated Dictionary of the Gods and Symbols of Ancient Mexico and the Maya*. (New York, NY: Thames & Hudson Inc., 1993). Pg. 176
40. Foster, Lynn V. *Handbook to Life in the Ancient Maya World*. (New York, NY: Oxford University Press, 2005). Pg. 193
41. "Lady Xoc." Wikipedia, the free encyclopedia. (November 19, 2011). http://en.wikipedia.org/wiki/Lady_Xoc
42. "Vision Serpent." Wikipedia, the free encyclopedia. (November 19, 2011). http://en.wikipedia.org/wiki/Vision_Serpent
43. "Bloodletting Ritual of Lady Xoc." National Gallery of Art. (November 19, 2011). www.nga.gov/exhibitions/2004/maya/womenatcourt-p2.htm
44. Pasztory, Esther. *Aztec Art*. (Norman, OK: University of Oklahoma Press, 1998). Pg. 82
45. Ibid., 82
46. Pasztory, Esther. *Aztec Art*. (Norman, OK: University of Oklahoma Press, 1998). Pg. 83
47. Ibid., 83
48. Macgillivray III, Allan. *The Venus Calendar Observatory at Aztec New Mexico*." (Bloomington, IN: AuthorHouse, 2010). Pg. 110
49. Phillips, Charles. *The Complete Illustrated History: Aztec & Maya*. (New York, NY: Metro Books, 2008). Pg. 167

50. Ibid., 167
51. Ibid., 167
52. Ibid., 167
53. "Ixchel." Wikipedia, the free encyclopedia. (November 19, 2011). http://en.wikipedia.org/wiki/Ixchel
54. Ibid, "Ixchel"
55. Ibid, "Ixchel"
56. Independent research (FAMSI) around the names and meanings of the four directions. Nicholas A. Hopkins and J. Kathryn Josserand. "Directions and Partitions in Maya World View." 2001. 11-20-2011. http://www.famsi.org/research/hopkins/DirectionalPartitions.pdf
57. "Ometecuhtli." Encyclopædia Britannica Online. (November 19, 2011). http://www.britannica.com/EBchecked/topic/428358/Ometecuhtli
58. Mary Miller and Karl Taube. *An Illustrated Dictionary of the Gods and Symbols of Ancient Mexico and the Maya.* (New York, NY: Thames & Hudson Inc., 1993). Pg. 184
59. Ibid., 184
60. "Great Goddess of Teotihuacan." Wikipedia, the free encyclopedia. (November 19, 2011). http://en.wikipedia.org/wiki/Great_Goddess_of_Teotihuacan
61. Calleman, Carl Johan. *The Mayan Calendar and the Transformation of Consciousness.* (Rochester, VT: Bear & Company, 2004). Pg. 21
62. Jenkins, John Major. *Galactic Alignment: the Transformation of Consciousness According to Mayan, Egyptian, and Vedic Traditions.* (Rochester, VT: Bear & Company, 2002). Pg. 18
63. Calleman, Carl Johan. *The Mayan Calendar and the Transformation of Consciousness.* (Rochester, VT: Bear & Company, 2004). Pg. 214-20
64. Phillips, Charles. *The Complete Illustrated History: Aztec & Maya.* (New York, NY: Metro Books, 2008). Pg. 216

Chapter 3

1. Jenkins, John Major. *Galactic Alignment: the Transformation of Consciousness According to Mayan, Egyptian, and Vedic Traditions.* (Rochester, VT: Bear & Company, 2002). Pg. 18
2. Ibid., 18
3. Calleman, Carl Johan. *The Purposeful Universe: How Quantum Theory and Mayan Cosmology Explain the Origin and Evolution of Life.* (Rochester, VT: Bear & Company, 2009). Pg. 29

Chapter 4

1. Bruce Scofield and Barry C. Orr. *How to Practice Mayan Astrology: The Tzolkin Calendar and Your Life Path.* (Rochester, 51 VT: Bear & Company, 2007). Pg. 8-9

Chapter 5

1. "Xiuhtecuhtli." Wikipedia, the free encyclopedia. (November 19, 2011). http://en.wikipedia.org/wiki/Xiuhtecuhtli
2. Ibid., 1
3. Mary Miller and Karl Taube. *An Illustrated Dictionary of the Gods and Symbols of Ancient Mexico and the Maya.* (New York, NY: Thames & Hudson Inc., 1993). Pg. 167
4. Ibid., 167
5. Mary Miller and Karl Taube. *An Illustrated Dictionary of the Gods and Symbols of Ancient Mexico and the Maya.* (New York, NY: Thames & Hudson Inc., 1993). Pg. 60
6. "Chalchiuhtlicue." Wikipedia, the free encyclopedia. (November 19, 2011). http://en.wikipedia.org/wiki/Chalchiuhtlicue

7. Ibid., 1
8. Mary Miller and Karl Taube. *An Illustrated Dictionary of the Gods and Symbols of Ancient Mexico and the Maya.* (New York, NY: Thames & Hudson Inc., 1993). Pg. 60
9. Ibid., 172
10. Ibid., 172
11. "Chalchiuhtlicue." Wikipedia, the free encyclopedia. (November 19, 2011). http://en.wikipedia.org/wiki/Tonatiuh
12. Ibid., 1
13. "Tlazolteotl." Wikipedia, the free encyclopedia. (November 19, 2011). http://en.wikipedia.org/wiki/Tlazolteotl
14. Mary Miller and Karl Taube. *An Illustrated Dictionary of the Gods and Symbols of Ancient Mexico and the Maya.* (New York, NY: Thames & Hudson Inc., 1993). Pg. 168
15. "Tlazolteotl." Wikipedia, the free encyclopedia. (November 19, 2011). http://en.wikipedia.org/wiki/Tlazolteotl
16. Ibid., 1
17. Ibid., 1
18. Mary Miller and Karl Taube. *An Illustrated Dictionary of the Gods and Symbols of Ancient Mexico and the Maya.* (New York, NY: Thames & Hudson Inc., 1993). Pg. 112
19. "Mictlantecuhtli." Wikipedia, the free encyclopedia. (November 19, 2011). http://en.wikipedia.org/wiki/Mictlantecuhtli
20. Mary Miller and Karl Taube. *An Illustrated Dictionary of the Gods and Symbols of Ancient Mexico and the Maya.* (New York, NY: Thames & Hudson Inc., 1993). Pg. 112
21. Ibid., 112
22. "Mictlantecuhtli." Wikipedia, the free encyclopedia. (November 19, 2011). http://en.wikipedia.org/wiki/Mictlantecuhtli
23. Ibid., 1
24. Ibid., 1
25. Pasztory, Esther. *Aztec Art.* (Norman, OK: University of Oklahoma Press, 1998). Pg. 58
26. "Cinteotl." Wikipedia, the free encyclopedia. (November 19, 2011). http://en.wikipedia.org/wiki/Cinteotl
27. Ibid., 1
28. Phillips, Charles. *The Complete Illustrated History: Aztec & Maya.* (New York, NY: Metro Books, 2008). Pg. 51
29. Mary Miller and Karl Taube. *An Illustrated Dictionary of the Gods and Symbols of Ancient Mexico and the Maya.* (New York, NY: Thames & Hudson Inc., 1993). Pg. 166
30. Ibid., 166
31. Ibid., 166
32. Phillips, Charles. *The Complete Illustrated History: Aztec & Maya.* (New York, NY: Metro Books, 2008). Pg. 157
33. "Tlaloc." Wikipedia, the free encyclopedia. (November 19, 2011). http://en.wikipedia.org/wiki/Tlaloc
34. Ibid., 1
35. Ibid., 1
36. Ibid., 1
37. "Tlalocan." Wikipedia, the free encyclopedia. (November 19, 2011). http://en.wikipedia.org/wiki/Tlalocan
38. Beezley, *Mexico in World History*, pg. 1, associates the White Tezcatlipoca with the East and Phillips, Aztec & Maya, pg. 148, associates the White Tezcatlipoca with the West
39. Mary Miller and Karl Taube. *An Illustrated Dictionary of the Gods and Symbols of Ancient Mexico and the Maya.* (New York, NY: Thames & Hudson Inc., 1993). Pg. 141
40. Ibid., 141
41. Ibid., 142
42. Carrasco, David. *Quetzalcoatl and the Irony of Empire: Myths and Prophecies in the Aztec Tradition.* (Chicago, IL: The University of Chicago Press, 1982). Pg. 2
43. Ibid., 174
44. "Quetzalcoatl." Wikipedia, the free encyclopedia. (November 19, 2011). http://en.wikipedia.org/wiki/Quetzalcoatl

45. "Quetzalcoatl." Myths and Legends of the World. 2001. Encyclopedia.com. (November 19, 2011). www.encyclopedia.com/doc/1G2-3490900408.html
46. Phillips, Charles. *The Complete Illustrated History: Aztec & Maya*. (New York, NY: Metro Books, 2008). Pg. 148
47. "Tezcatlipoca." Wikipedia, the free encyclopedia. (November 19, 2011). http://en.wikipedia.org/wiki/Tezcatlipoca
48. Ibid., 1
49. Phillips, Charles. *The Complete Illustrated History: Aztec & Maya*. (New York, NY: Metro Books, 2008). Pg. 178
50. Calleman, Carl Johan. *The Purposeful Universe: How Quantum Theory and Mayan Cosmology Explain the Origin and Evolution of Life*. (Rochester, VT: Bear & Company, 2009). Pg. 320
51. "Metztli." Wikipedia, the free encyclopedia. (November 19, 2011). http://en.wikipedia.org/wiki/Metztli
52. Ibid., 1
53. Spence, Lewis. *The Myths of Mexico and Peru*. (New York, NY: Dover Publications, 1995). Pg. 77
54. Mary Miller and Karl Taube. *An Illustrated Dictionary of the Gods and Symbols of Ancient Mexico and the Maya*. (New York, NY: Thames & Hudson Inc., 1993). Pg. 166
55. Ibid., 166
56. Ibid., 166
57. Ibid., 166
58. Orlando O. Espin and James B. Nickoloff. *An Introductory Dictionary of Theology and Religious Studies*. (Collegeville, MN: Liturgical Press, 2007). Pg. 932
59. Phillips, Charles. *The Complete Illustrated History: Aztec & Maya*. (New York, NY: Metro Books, 2008). Pg. 176, 215
60. Mary Miller and Karl Taube. *An Illustrated Dictionary of the Gods and Symbols of Ancient Mexico and the Maya*. (New York, NY: Thames & Hudson Inc., 1993). Pg. 127
61. Ibid., 127
62. "Ometeotl." Wikipedia, the free encyclopedia. (November 19, 2011). http://en.wikipedia.org/wiki/Ometeotl
63. "Five Suns." Wikipedia, the free encyclopedia. (November 19, 2011). http://en.wikipedia.org/wiki/Five_Suns

Chapter 6

1. Calleman, Carl Johan. *Solving the Great Mystery of Our Time: The Mayan Calendar*. (London: Garev Publishing, 2001)
2. Calleman, Carl Johan. *The Mayan Calendar and the Transformation of Consciousness*. (Rochester, VT: Bear & Company, 2004). Pg.146

Chapter 7

1. Calleman, Carl Johan. *The Mayan Calendar and the Transformation of Consciousness*. (Rochester, VT: Bear & Company, 2004). Pg. 24-35
2. Phillips, Charles. *The Complete Illustrated History: Aztec & Maya*. (New York, NY: Metro Books, 2008). Pg. 142
3. Jenkins, John Major. *Maya Cosmogenesis 2012*. (Rochester, VT: Bear & Company, 1998). Pg. 117

Chapter 8

1. Pasztory, Esther. *Aztec Art*. (Norman, OK: University of Oklahoma Press, 1998). Pg. 213
2. Jenkins, John Major. *Galactic Alignment: the Transformation of Consciousness According to Mayan, Egyptian, and Vedic Traditions*.

(Rochester, VT: Bear & Company, 2002). Pg. 29-30
3. Phillips, Charles. *The Complete Illustrated History: Aztec & Maya*. (New York, NY: Metro Books, 2008). Pg. 218-19
4. Mary Miller and Karl Taube. *An Illustrated Dictionary of the Gods and Symbols of Ancient Mexico and the Maya*. (New York, NY: Thames & Hudson Inc., 1993). Pg. 84
5. Ibid., 74.
6. David Freidel, Linda Schele, and Joy Parker. *Maya Cosmos: Three Thousand Years on the Shaman's Path*. (New York, NY: William Morrow and Company, 1993). Pg. 180
7. Ibid., 188.
8. Mary Miller and Karl Taube. *An Illustrated Dictionary of the Gods and Symbols of Ancient Mexico and the Maya*. (New York, NY: Thames & Hudson Inc., 1993). Pg. 84
9. Ibid., 85
10. Ibid., 84
11. Ibid., 85
12. Jenkins, John Major. *Galactic Alignment: the Transformation of Consciousness According to Mayan, Egyptian, and Vedic Traditions*. (Rochester, VT: Bear & Company, 2002). Pg. 20
13. Ibid., 71
14. Ibid., 25
15. "A Young Pulsar Shows Its Hand." NASA Image of the Day Gallery. (November 19, 2011). www.nasa.gov/multimedia/imagegallery/image_feature_1323.html
16. David Freidel, Linda Schele, and Joy Parker. *Maya Cosmos: Three Thousand Years on the Shaman's Path*. (New York, NY: William Morrow and Company, 1993). Pg. 182-84
17. Ibid., 182
18. Ibid., 182
19. Ibid., 66-67
20. Ibid., 75
21. Ibid., 183
22. Ibid., 256
23. Ibid., 184
24. Mary Miller and Karl Taube. *An Illustrated Dictionary of the Gods and Symbols of Ancient Mexico and the Maya*. (New York, NY: Thames & Hudson Inc., 1993). Pg. 186
25. Calleman, Carl Johan. *The Mayan Calendar and the Transformation of Consciousness*. (Rochester, VT: Bear & Company, 2004). Pg. 34-36
26. David Freidel, Linda Schele, and Joy Parker. *Maya Cosmos: Three Thousand Years on the Shaman's Path*. (New York, NY: William Morrow and Company, 1993). Pg. 53
27. Ibid., 256

Bibliography

Andrews, Synthia and Colin Andrews. *The Complete Idiot's Guide© to 2012: An Ancient Look at a Critical Time.* (New York, NY: The Penguin Group, 2008).

Archology. *Secrets of the Maya: Histoire du Mexique* (Long Island City, NY: Hatherleigh Press, 2004).

Beezley, William H. *Mexico in World History* (New Oxford World History). (New York, NY: Oxford University Press, 2011).

Brennan, Martin. *The Hidden Maya: A New Understanding of Maya Glyphs.* (Rochester, VT: Bear & Company, 1998).

Calleman, Carl Johan. *The Mayan Calendar and the Transformation of Consciousness.* (Rochester, VT: Bear & Company, 2004).

Calleman, Carl Johan. *Solving the Great Mystery of Our Time: The Mayan Calendar.* (London: Garev Publishing, 2001).

Calleman, Carl Johan. *The Purposeful Universe: How Quantum Theory and Mayan Cosmology Explain the Origin and Evolution of Life.* (Rochester, VT: Bear & Company, 2009).

Carrasco, David. *Quetzalcoatl and the Irony of Empire: Myths and Prophecies in the Aztec Tradition.* (Chicago, IL: The University of Chicago Press, 1982).

Clow, Barbara Hand. *The Mayan Code: Time Acceleration and Awakening the World Mind.* (Rochester, VT: Bear & Company, 2007).

Coe, Michael D. *Breaking the Maya Code.* (London: Thames & Hudson, Inc., 1992).

Coe, Michael D. and Rex Koontz. *Mexico: From the Olmecs to the Aztecs.* (New York, NY: Thames & Hudson Inc., 2008).

"Corn Deities and the Complementary Male/Female Principle." Bassie-Sweet, Karen. Mesoweb.com. (November 19, 2011). www.mesoweb.com/features/bassie/corn/media/corn_deities.pdf.

Espin, Orlando O. and James B. Nickoloff. *An Introductory Dictionary of Theology and Religious Studies.* (Collegeville, MN: Liturgical Press, 2007).

Foster, Lynn V. *Handbook to Life in the Ancient Maya World.* (New York, NY: Oxford University Press, 2005).

Freidel, David, Linda Schele, and Joy Parker. *Maya Cosmos: Three Thousand Years on the Shaman's Path.* (New York, NY: William Morrow and Company, 1993).

Gilbert, Adrian. *2012: Mayan Year of Destiny.* (Virginia Beach, VA: A.R.E. Press, 2006).

"Glyphs G and F: Identified as Aspects of the Maize God." Gronemeyer, Sven. WAYEB Notes (ISSN: 1379-8286, 2003). www.wayeb.org.

Hancock, Graham. *Fingerprints of the Gods.* (New York, NY: Crown Publishers, 1995).

Harrison, Peter D. *The Lords of Tikal: Rulers of an Ancient Maya City.* (New York, NY: Thames and Hudson, Inc., 2000).

"Histoyre du méchique." 1905, ed. E. de Jonghe. *Journal de la Société des Americanistes*, N.S., 1-42. Hopkins, Nicholas A. and J. Kathryn Josserand. "Directions and Partitions in Maya World View." 2001. 11-20-2011. http://www.famsi.org/research/hopkins/DirectionalPartitions.pdf

"Is the Sun Emitting a Mystery Particle?" O'Neil, Ian. *Discovery News* (2010). http://news.discovery.com/space/is-the-sunemitting-a-mystery-particle.html.

Jenkins, John Major. *Maya Cosmogenesis 2012.* (Rochester, VT: Bear & Company, 1998).

Jenkins, John Major. *Galactic Alignment: the Transformation of Consciousness According to Mayan, Egyptian, and Vedic Traditions.* (Rochester, VT: Bear & Company, 2002).

Joseph, Lawrence E. *Apocalypse 2012: Investigation into Civilization's End.* (New York, NY: Broadway Books, 2008).

Leon-Portilla, Miguel. *Aztec Thought and Culture: A Study of the Ancient Nahuatl Mind.* Translated by Jack Emory Davis. (Norman, OK: University of Oklahoma Press, 1990).

Macgillivray III, Allan. *The Venus Calendar Observatory at Aztec New Mexico.*" (Bloomington, IN: AuthorHouse, 2010).

"Mayan Calendar: The World will not End, The." Barrios, Carlos. Maya

Mystery School (2011). http://www.mayamysteryschool.com.

Men, Hunbatz. *Secrets of Mayan Science/Religion.* (Rochester, VT: Bear & Company, 1990).

Meyer, Karl E. *Teotihuacán.* (New York, NY: Newsweek: Wonders of Man Series, 1973).

Miller, Mary and Karl Taube. *An Illustrated Dictionary of the Gods and Symbols of Ancient Mexico and the Maya.* (New York, NY: Thames & Hudson Inc., 1993).

Montgomery, John. *How to Read Maya Hieroglyphs.* (New York, NY: Hippocrene Books, Inc., 2002).

National Geographic, Collector's Edition. "Mysteries of the Maya: the rise, glory and collapse of an ancient civilization." (Washington, D.C.: National Geographic Society, 2008).

Page, Christine R. *2012 and the Galactic Center: The Return of the Great Mother.* (Rochester, VT: Bear & Company, 2008).

Pasztory, Esther. *Aztec Art.* (Norman, OK: University of Oklahoma Press, 1998).

Phillips, Charles. *The Illustrated Encyclopedia of Aztec & Maya: the History, Legend, Myth and Culture of the Ancient Native Peoples of Mexico and Central America.* (London, England: Lorenz Books, 2004).

Phillips, Charles. *The Complete Illustrated History: Aztec & Maya.* (New York, NY: Metro Books, 2008).

Popol Vuh: The Sacred Book of the Ancient Quiche Maya. (English version by Delia Goetz and S. G. Morley from the translation by Adrian Recinos) (Norman, OK: University of Oklahoma Press, 1991).

"Popol Vuh Relief—El Mirador, Guatemala." Zorich, Zach. *Archaeology,* Vol. 63 No.1 (January/February, 2010) http://archaeology.org/1001/topten/guatemala.html.

Schellhas, Paul. *Representation of Deities of the Maya Manuscripts – Papers of the Peabody Museum of American Archaeology and Ethnology.* eBook: #18013 (Harvard University, Vol. 4, No. 1, 2006) (http://www.gutenberg.org).

Scofield, Bruce and Barry C. Orr. *How to Practice Mayan Astrology: The Tzolkin Calendar and Your Life Path.* (Rochester, VT: Bear & Company, 2007).

Spence, Lewis. *The Myths of Mexico and Peru.* (New York, NY: Dover Publications, 1995).

"Strange Case of Solar Flares and Radioactive Elements, The." Strober, Dan. (Stanford Report, 2010.) http://news.stanford.edu/news/2010/august/sun-082310.html.

Stross, Brian. "Maize in Word and Image in Southeastern Mesoamerica." (University of Texas Academic Press, 2006).

Internet Resources

Calleman, Carl Johan (http://www.calleman.com).

FAMSI, Foundation for the Advancement of Mesoamerican Studies, Inc. (http://famsi.org).

Mayan Calendar Portal (www.mayancalendarportal.com).

MESOWEB. This site features Mesoamerica and its cultures including Maya, Aztec, and Olmec. (www.mesoweb.com).

WAYEB, European Association of Mayanists (www.wayeb.org).

Project Gutenberg, the first producer of free eBooks. (www.gutenberg.org/wiki/Main_{age_).

About the Authors Artists

Patricia A. Padilla

A native New Mexican, Patricia Padilla was born into eight generations of Curanderas—an age-old Hispanic healing tradition. She ran her own alternative medical clinic in Lyons, Colorado, serving the community as an acupuncturist and herbalist for twenty years. She also published and wrote for a local weekly newspaper for twenty-four years.

Patricia lives near Taos where she continues to work with people, write, and paint. She provides workshops, classes, seminars, and articles about Curanderas topics, as well showing in galleries. Look for her upcoming work chronicling her life's story as a Curandera and a novel about flamenco.

For more information about Patricia's work, visit her blog at: http://curanderapadilla.wordpress.com.

Marlena V. Freelove

A child of immigrant parents, Marlena Freelove traveled the roads of the Midwest during childhood with her father, from Post-WWII Germany, and her mother, from the Lake Patzcuaro Basin, Michoacán, Mexico, until they settled in Boulder, Colorado in 1962. In 1976, she began her computer career through a government-sponsored program and continued in that field for the next twenty years in a variety of positions from operator to micro computer specialist.

At the age of 38, after surviving a serious car accident, she began to live a dual life of professional and spiritual seeker. Her path eventually led her to the small, busy clinic at the back of the *Lyons Newspaper* office and into a lifetime friendship with co-author Patricia Padilla.

Marlena lives near Taos, where she continues to write and create art with a variety of paint, collage, and assemblage techniques, and now uses the computer for creative expression. She has worked with a variety of magazines, blogs, and shows in galleries.

For more information about her work, visit Marlena's blog at: http://marlenafreelove.wordpress.com.

INDEX

Adjustment
Adjustment, 39-40, 148
Alchemy, 153
Ancestors, 28, 38, 50, 117, 152, 154-155
Archetype, 52, 175, 178
Big Dipper, 46
Cellular, 130
Centzon Totochtin, 24
Chac, 115
Chalchiuhtlicue, 29-30, 104-105
Chariot, 37-38
Chichén Itza, 128, 158
Childbirth, 58, 104, 121
Chimalmat, 46
Chorti, 58
Cinteotl, 112-113
Creation, 60, 144, 165-166, 170, 194
  Gods of, 34, 117, 119, 124, 125
  Story of, 13, 56, 58, 107, 111, 117, 119, 155
Day, 15, 48, 74-95
Death, 47-48, 80, 81, 101, 109, 110, 111
Devil, 51-52
Earth Monster, 51-52
East, 60, 75, 107
Eclipse, 48, 157-158
Ehecatl-Quetzalcoatl, 117
Emperor, 31-32
Empress, 29-30, 191
Familial, 76, 132
Fertility, 48, 54, 64, 111, 117
Fifth Element, 18
Fifth Sun, 107
Fire/Water/Stream, 53-54
First Father, 68-71
Fool, 23-24
Fortune, 41-42
Four Directions, 15, 58, 60, 75, 144-148, 170

Galactic, 129, 138-139
Global, 137-138
Hand of God, 159-160
Hanged Man, 45-46
Hero Twins, 42, 46, 56
Hierophant, 33-34
Hopi Palulukong, 117
Huitzilopochtli, 13, 66, 125
Hunab K'u, 14, 15, 17, 22, 39, 170
Hunahpu, 46, 70
Intercession, 15, 152-170
Itztlacoliuhqui-Ixquimilli, 123
Ix Chel, 57-58
Jaguar, 28, 42, 62, 78, 89, 115, 119, 128, 148
King Bird Jaguar, 31-32
King Pacal, 32
Kukulcan, 38, 128, 158
La Reina, 161-162
Lady Xoc, 27-28, 50
Lamat, 55-56, 83
Law Giver, 39-40
Little Dipper, 46
Lovers, 35-36
Lust, 43-44, 52, 109
Magus, 25-26
Maize God, 41-42, 105, 166
Mammalian, 131
Mayahuel, 29
Mictlan, 22, 111, 117
Mictlantecuhtli, 110-111
Midwives, 48, 58, 108, 109
Milky Way, 12, 16, 17, 58, 70, 144, 166, 169, 170
Moon, 42, 56, 57-58, 90, 99, 120, 121, 157, 165, 192
morning star, 38, 56, 117, 122, 123
Na goddess, 42
National, 135-136
Nawal, 22, 163-164
New Fire Ceremony, 48
North, 60, 75, 119, 125, 145

Ometecuhtli, 35-36, 101, 111, 125
Ometeotl, 22, 60, 66, 124-125, 183
Orion, 165-167, 194, 196, 198
Our Lady of Guadalupe, 161-162
Overworld, 15, 26, 62, 74, 98-125, 144, 170, 175, 193
Patecatl, 23-24
Pax god, 42
penitential rites, 44
Tonatiuh, 106-107
Tower, 53-54
Tribal, 133-134
Turtle, 42, 62, 154, 165, 194
Tzitzimitl, 47-48
Tzolkin, 13, 17, 74
Tzotzil Maya, 58
Underworld, 15, 22, 28, 37, 57-58, 60, 62, 64, 74, 85, 98-99, 111, 128-140, 144, 147-148, 170, 175, 190, 195
Universal, 40, 140
Universe, 13, 14, 22, 63-64, 115, 125, 144, 180
Venus, 38, 56, 83, 123
Vision, 22, 28, 50, 114
Vision Serpent, 28, 49-50
War, 34, 38, 54, 56, 99, 114, 115, 119, 125
Warriors, 34, 50, 106
Water Lily, 42, 61-62
West, 60, 75, 125, 148
White Flower, 167-168
World Tree, 16-17, 144, 154, 166, 167, 169-170, 180
Xiuhtecuhtli, 100-101, 193, 196
Xochiquetzal, 64, 65-66, 183
Xolotl, 111
Yaxchilan, 28, 50
Yohualticitl, 120-121
Yucatec, 38, 58
Zuni Kolowisi, 117

Zuni Kolowisi, 117
Pleiades, 113, 158
Priestess, 27-28, 184
Quetzalcoatl, 13, 37-38, 56, 59-60, 103, 111, 113, 115, 116-117, 119, 123, 125, 158
Quetzalpalotl, 26,
Regional, 134
Sacrifice, 56, 81, 121, 145, 154
  Blood of, 12, 28, 50
  Human, 38, 107, 115, 117
Scorpion, 44
Self Love, 65-66, 183
Seven Macaw, 45-46
sin-eater, 44
Smoking Mirror, 33-34, 118-119
South, 60, 66, 75, 125, 146, 189, 195
Star, 55-56
Star Road, 12, 17, 169, 170, 175
Stillness, 61-62
Sun, 42, 46, 48, 52, 56, 59-60, 95, 106, 107, 115, 121, 123, 157, 175
Tamoanchan, 66
Teotihuacán, 26, 64, 123
Teotihuacán Spider Woman, 63-64
Tezcatlipoca, 34, 56, 103, 117, 118-119, 125
Tikal, 128
Tlahuizcalpantecuhtli, 122-123
Tlaloc, 30, 114-115, 117
Tlalocan, 115
Tlaltecuhtli, 102-103
Tlazolteotl, 43-44, 108-109
Tollan, 38, 107, 117
Tolpiltzin Quetzalcoatl, 38, 117
Tonatiuh, 106-107
Tower, 53-54